Register of Research in Special Education in the United Kingdom

Volume One: 1983−4

Prepared for publication by
SEAMUS HEGARTY
with assistance from Janet May-Bowles
and Linda McCreery

We gratefully acknowledge advice and assistance received from Annette
Mendelssohn, Stephen Pickles and Klaus Wedell.

NFER-NELSON

Published by The NFER-NELSON Publishing Company Ltd.,
Darville House, 2 Oxford Road East,
Windsor, Berkshire SL4 1DF, England
and
242 Cherry Street, Philadelphia, PA 19106-1906.
Tel: (215) 238 0939. Telex: 244489.

First Published 1986
© 1986 National Foundation for Educational Research in England and Wales

Library of Congress Cataloging in Publication data is available.

Filmsetting by Vantage Photosetting Co Ltd
Eastleigh and London
Printed by Billing & Sons Limited, Worcester.

ISBN 0 7005 1002 8
Code 8236 02 1

Contents

How to use the Register

The main Register entries are arranged alphabetically according to the name of the institution initiating the research. Within each institution, the entries are arranged alphabetically by college, if applicable, then by department, and then by researcher. Each entry, in addition, is consecutively numbered (from 1/001 to 1/178).

Name and subject indexes appear at the back of the volume. The subject index is based on the Keywords which appear at the end of each Register entry, and each entry is listed against all of its Keywords.

This work was supported by a grant from the Economic and Social Research Council but the content is the sole responsibility of the copyright holder.

Introduction

Background

Recent years have seen a modest blossoming of research in special education in the United Kingdom. There have been major funded studies on integration, different aspects of curriculum, children with specific learning difficulties, the situation of adolescents, the educational implications of various handicapping conditions and other topics. These have been matched by a growth in research activity based on schools or undertaken by individual teachers and academics. Student theses and dissertations are increasingly addressing topics relating to special needs in education.

Encouraging though these developments are, they are beset by a major weakness which could negate much of the benefit to be gained from the research effort, viz. inadequate dissemination. This is not peculiar to the United Kingdom or to special education as an area of inquiry. An American study of research on education for the handicapped over a 12-year period found the bulk of the research involved discrete projects of short duration spread across a large number of institutions; there was little or no evidence of educational benefit from 'this diverse shotgun approach' (CRC, 1976). More generally, it is fair to say that one of the less impressive things about educational research – and other social sciences research for that matter – is the steps taken to disseminate it.

Dissemination of research findings in special education is made peculiarly difficult by the 'cottage industry' nature of much of the research enterprise. A great many studies are done in academic isolation as part requirement for a degree or in spare time squeezed out from teaching commitments. Individuals ploughing their own furrows in this way inevitably see the completion of the study as their major goal and tend to give low priority to disseminating any findings. In any case, they do not usually have the resources to translate research findings into strategies for change or engage in appropriate dialogue with practitioners.

Effective dissemination is important in special education research for a number of reasons. Resources for work in this area are limited, all the more so in the light of the complexity and the heterogeneity of the issues at stake. Wasteful overlap and duplication of effort must therefore be avoided wherever possible. More positively, it is essential to capitalize on scarce resources by pooling research findings, ensuring that new projects take account of and build upon earlier studies, and by promoting collaborative research efforts. In the end, what matters is the effect on practice. If the research enterprise is to be justified, information on findings must be made widely available so as to facilitate practitioners in bringing about useful change.

Some information on special education research is picked up in existing registers of research. The NFER Register of Educational Research in the United Kingdom, the Newcastle Polytechnic Directory of non-medical research relating to Handicapped People, and certain medical and other registers all contain relevant entries. This is certainly useful, not least in bringing special education issues to wider audiences, but the listings are incomplete and, because of the presence of extraneous material, searching is made inefficient when the concern is exclusively with special education. What is needed therefore is something that collects all or most of the scattered information into one place and confines itself to special education. These are the aims of the present enterprise. This is only one stage in the dissemination process but it is an essential one.

Collecting the information

An earlier SSRC-funded study provided a convenient starting point. This was conducted by Klaus Wedell and Jenny Roberts at the University of London Institute of Education in 1981 and sought to collect information on United Kingdom research on children with special educational needs. The present study aimed in the first instance to repeat the Wedell/Roberts survey and bring this information up to date. It has also endeavoured to establish procedures for updating the information on a regular basis and for disseminating it as widely as possible.

The information was collected by means of a questionnaire dispatched in Spring/Summer 1984. This followed the pattern of the Wedell/Roberts questionnaire but was constructed so as to provide information which matched the Council of Europe EUDISED format. A UNESCO definition of special education was given for guidance: *a form of education provided for those who were not achieving, or are unlikely to achieve, through ordinary educational provision the levels of educational, social and other attainments appropriate to their age and which has the aim of furthering their progress towards these levels.* In addition, categories of relevant research were outlined and illustrated with examples.

The questionnaire was sent to universities, polytechnics, colleges of higher education, local education authorities, and other bodies and individuals considered likely to be engaged in relevant research. Letters publicizing the survey appeared in the *Times Educational Supplement*, the *Times Higher Education Supplement, Special Education: Forward Trends* and *Education Guardian*, and further questionnaires were dispatched to inquirers responding to this publicity. More than two hundred completed questionnaires were returned. While this was a small proportion of the questionnaires dispatched, it does in fact represent a satisfactory outcome: most of the responses elicited through the follow-up procedures were simply to confirm a nil response; and, additionally, responses were obtained from all locations known to be engaged in relevant research.

Presentation of findings

The aim has been to cover all current research in special education in the United Kingdom. Because this is the first published register in the series, 'current' has been extended to take in work completed in 1983. A number of responses which featured earlier completion dates were excluded. Excluded also were responses which could not be regarded as research even with a very broad definition of research, e.g. staff development initiatives, or which fell outside special education, e.g. drugs education studies.

The findings have been indexed by means of keywords. The initial intention had been to use a thesaurus base. (The draft special education subthesarus of the EUDISED Multilingual Thesaurus was adapted for UK use by adding in terms from the unpublished register of research prepared by Wedell and Roberts.) Because of the small number of entries, however, and the fact that a computerized database could not be set up, it was decided that a thesaurus base would be too cumbersome and would not offer users the most convenient way of gaining access to the information in the register.

The initial questionnaire had asked researchers to propose keywords that could be used to describe their research. These have been retained for use here wherever possible, hence the presence of keywords such as ESN which though outmoded in terms of the Education

Act 1981 is still in use. Considerable re-working of the keywords has been necessary in order to describe studies with due precision, to ensure that keyword terms are used in a compatible way and to employ the minimum number of terms consonant with adequate specificity. This re-working has taken account of current thinking and terminology in special education. The net result has been that many studies have been described and indexed either wholly or partly by terms other than those initially proposed for them.

Reference

CRC (1976). *Twelve years of research on education for the handicapped.* Belmont, MA: Contract Research Corporation.

SEAMUS HEGARTY

Aston University

1/001   LDU
Applied Psychology
College House
University of Aston
Birmingham B4 7ET

Chambers, Michael
Supervisor: Newton, Margaret, Dr

A study of alternative CNS information processing systems in relation to the dyslexia syndrome.

Background: A study into the neuropsychological aspects of the developmental dyslexia syndrome, with particular emphasis on right hemisphere functioning and lexical processing.

Design: Essentially, an investigation into the visuo–spatial reasoning abilities, visual retention and recall of abstract cyphers, and lexical processing in the developmental dyslexic.

Size: Various; usually 25–50.

Methods: Various: battery of standardized spatial ability tests; visual retention experiments; word recognition experiments; microcomputer-based reaction time experiments.

Date of Research: October 1981–Summer 1986.

KEYWORDS: dyslexia; information processing; central nervous system

1/002   Department of Educational Enquiry
University of Aston
Gosta Green
Birmingham B4 7ET

Thompson, M., Dr; Barnard, A., Mrs
Supervisor: Whitfield, R. C., Prof.

Screening for early educational difficulties.

Background: To investigate ways of identifying young children who might encounter reading, writing and spelling difficulties at a later stage.

Size: 229 children taken from four state schools in one health authority area; mean age at first testing 4.8 years.

Methods: Children were screened at four to five years and tested again two years later by means of a battery of standardized tests covering reading, spelling, writing and non-verbal reasoning.

Results: Most correlations were low and non-significant. Most of the pre-school screening items were found not to predict to subsequent reading, spelling or writing performance.

Date of Research: 1981–1983.

Published Material: BARNARD, A., COMBER, L.C. and THOMPSON, M.E. (1983). *Screening for Early Educational Difficulties: A Review of Procedures and a Pilot Case Study at Preschool Level.* Birmingham: University of Aston.

KEYWORDS: pre-school; screening; assessment; reading; writing; spelling

Avery Hill College of Education

1/003   Avery Hill College   Oliver, Mike, Dr
          Bexley Road
          London SE9 2PQ
          Tel: 01-850-0081

Innovation and change in relation to children with special educational needs.

Background: The Warnock Report and the Education Act 1981 have had profound effects upon the whole schooling process and in particular upon the meeting of special needs within ordinary schools. In order better to understand some of the processes involved, the possible effects and the implication for the education system as a whole, two schools have been studied in depth: a school for deaf children which is shortly to be integrated with an adjacent primary school and an ordinary secondary school. The context in which this research is taking place follows from Warnock's recommendations that colleges should act increasingly as resource and co-ordinating centres for teacher- and school-based research. In addition the research will relate to existing teaching programmes and possible future higher degree and INSET courses.
Methods: Action research.

Date of Research: September 1983–Summer 1987.

KEYWORDS: integration; hearing impairment; resource centre; teacher-based research

Banstead Place Assessment Centre

1/004   Banstead Place Assessment Centre   Simms, Barbara, Mrs (Ed.
          Park Road   psychologist); Parkinson,
          Banstead   Margaret, Mrs (Orthoptist)
          Surrey SM7 3EE
          Tel: 07373–51674

Visual disorders, visual–perceptual performance and educational attainment in the young disabled: a pilot study.

Background: A considerable number of those with physical disabilities, particularly congenital disabilities associated with neurological impairment, e.g. spina bifida with hydrocephalus, cerebral palsy, in addition demonstrate visual disorders such as nystagmus, squint, weak binocular function and visual field defects. The majority of such individuals are also subject to routine psychological assessments to determine the most suitable school or post-school placements. Those with visual defects may therefore be at a disadvantage when faced with visual–perceptual tests when poor performance may be regarded as an indication of limited learning ability rather than a reflection of a more fundamental visual disorder.
Design: The aim of this study is to determine the relationship between visual disorders and visual–perceptual performance and the effects on educational attainment.
Size: Students at Banstead Place Assessment Centre for Disabled School Leavers are routinely seen by a psychologist and orthoptist on admission. Fifty students aged 16–20 years with a diagnosis of cerebral palsy or spina bifida with hydrocephalus will be administered a battery of visual–perceptual and visual tests (including specific tests to determine eye movements) together with measures of educational attainment. The test

results will be analysed to determine the degree of correlation between the visual disorders, perceptual difficulties and level of educational attainment.

Results: It is expected that those with certain visual disorders will perform poorly on visual–perceptual performance tests and that these individuals will be particularly poor achievers educationally.

Date of Research: June 1984–June 1986.

KEYWORDS: visual impairment; visual perception; physical handicap; assessment; educational attainment

Banstead Place Mobility Centre

1/005   Banstead Place Mobility Centre   Simms, Barbara, Mrs (Ed.
         Park Road   psychologist); Dance, Anthony
         Banstead   (Driving instructor)
         Surrey SM7 3EE
         Tel: 07373-51674

The young disabled driver: perceptual-cognitive skills and 'on-road' performance during driving tuition.

Background: Driving tuition can be a lengthy and frustrating activity for the able-bodied, and for those with a physical handicap which involves some degree of brain damage, e.g. spina bifida with hydrocephalus, cerebral palsy, the difficulties can seem insurmountable. Driving ability assessment at Banstead Place Mobility Centre provides an in-depth analysis of an individual's suitability for driving and the car adaptations required. Based on psychological testing, recommendations are also made concerning the kinds of learning and 'on road' difficulties likely to be encountered. The aim of this study is to determine the predictive validity of psychological test results for 'on road' difficulties throughout driving tuition.
Size: Twelve disabled students residential at Banstead Place Assessment Centre (aged 16–20 years) of mixed disabilities, who have been assessed as suitable candidates for driving tuition.
Methods: All students will be given at least one hour's 'in-car' driving tuition per week by a qualified instructor experienced in teaching the disabled to drive. After *each* ten hours' tuition, each student will be taken on a set local route, throughout which his driving performance will be rated on a checklist by two trained observers. This procedure will be repeated until each student takes and passes his driving test. The correlation between the types of errors made during driving tuition and performance on psychological tests assessing visual discrimination, visual scanning and tracking, figure–ground discrimination, logical reasoning and deduction, spatial ability, left–right orientation, learning and memory ability (given during the driving ability assessment prior to tuition) will be investigated. It is hoped that this analysis will enable predictions to be made concerning the difficulties likely to be experienced by the young disabled driver and thus offer information of value to the driving instructor.

Date of Research: January 1984–December 1985.

KEYWORDS: perceptual–cognitive skill; physical handicap; neurological damage; driving tuition

Bath University

1/006   School of Education   Harper, Eon, Dr; Craft, Ann, Mrs
         University of Bath
         Claverton Down
         Bath BA2 7AY
         Tel: 0225-61244

Health Education for Slow Learners Project: evaluation of the training and aftercare phase.

Background: The evaluation is monitoring the training and aftercare phase of the Health Education for Slow Learners Project, the aims of which are to develop a training programme and training material to help teachers plan and implement health education of slow learning pupils (age range 5–16).
Design: The evaluation is supportive, providing a formative component, and critical. It will identify strengths and weaknesses of the process of training and dissemination of 'Fit For Life' materials. A number of interim reports and a final evaluation report will be produced.
Methods: Structured interviews with key personnel, including trainers and teachers; document analysis; questionnaires.

Date of Research: January 1983–December 1985.

KEYWORDS: health education; slow learner; programme evaluation

Bedford College of Higher Education

1/007   Bedford College of Higher Education   Harnett, Peter R.H. (School of
         Landsdowne Road   Education)
         Bedford MK40   *Supervisors:* Harnett, Peter; Lee,
         Tel: 0234-517966   Martin, Dr (School of Human
                                                Movement Studies); Gammage,
                                                P., Prof. (Nottingham University)

Investigation into anxiety in children who have special educational needs and strategies that schools and teachers adopt that affect such anxiety.

Background: Ethnographic study of children manifesting problems of learning and behaviour in mainstream schools, using a theoretical framework based on the theories of Harry Stack Sullivan. Anxiety is viewed from a psychodynamic, yet social psychological standpoint and is seen as an interpersonal phenomenon. The study is particularly interested in looking at the ways in which anxiety manifests itself in children and the ways that this affects their ability to learn in the classroom.
Methods: Ethnographic – case study using informal observation, structured and unstructured interviews within the context of participant observation.

Date of Research: January 1984–October 1986.

KEYWORDS: anxiety; behaviour problem; learning difficulties

Queen's University of Belfast

1/008   Department of Psychology   Mack, Pamela, Mrs (Dept. of
             Queen's University of Belfast   Child Psychiatry, Royal Belfast
             Belfast BT7 1NN   Hospital for Sick Children)
                                        Supervisor: Trew, Karen, Dr

Child behaviour problems: an investigation of treatment variables and therapeutic outcome.

Background: The background research is very large with most work to date being carried out in the USA. Parent management training has been shown to be an effective treatment for conduct disordered children. However, many families drop out at baseline and during treatment, and refuse to complete follow up. This study looks in detail at variables influencing treatment, within the family, environment and the target child him/herself. The parents' individual views of treatment progress, skills they are using, and influencing variables are monitored. The parents' views of each other's progress are also monitored with regard to the latter.

Design: The research data is collected at the following stages: baseline/1 month after treatment starts/3 months/every subsequent 3 months until termination/6 month follow up.

Size: Minimum 18 treatment cases, 25 to date involved in the study. Age range 3 years to 7.11 years. Male and female conduct disordered children. Screening out developmental delays (indicative of mental retardation), physical handicap, organic factors (epilepsy, brain damage etc), speech and language delay and previously treated families. Single parent and two parent families are included.

Methods: Eyeberg child behaviour inventory; Robinson/Eyeberg diadic coding system; Eyeberg therapy attitude inventory; parent report data; therapy progress rating scale for parents and therapist (Pamela Mack); parent manual (Pamela Mack).

Date of Research: January 1983–July/September 1985.

KEYWORDS: conduct disorder; behaviour problem; family; parent training

1/009   Department of Psychology   Mack, Pamela, Mrs (Dept. of
             Queen's University of Belfast   Child Psychiatry, Royal Belfast
             Belfast BT7 1NN   Hospital for Sick Children)
                                          Supervisor: Trew, Karen, Dr

A normal study of child behaviour in Belfast: getting norms for the Eyeberg child behaviour inventory.

Background: To obtain norms for the Eyeberg child behaviour inventory in Belfast a family information sheet compiled by Elliott and Mack in 1983 has been designed to obtain relevant family, child and environment data which will influence interpretation of data and screening of appropriate subjects. It is hoped that this behaviour inventory in association with the family information sheet will be used as screening tools for primary care teams and as treatment guides/diagnostic tools for clinicians in the conduct disordered field.

Design: 500–600 children in Belfast are being screened *randomly* by health visitors. The parent completes the inventory and the health visitor completes the family information sheet, along with the parent.

Size: 500–600 children resident in Belfast aged 3 years to 7–11 years.

Methods: Eyeberg child behaviour inventory. Family information sheet (Elliott & Mack, 1983).

Date of Research: August 1983 – July/September 1985.

KEYWORDS: *behaviour inventory; conduct disorder; screening; checklist*

Birmingham Polytechnic

1/010   National Centre for Down's   Brinkworth, Rex, (National
         Syndrome   Centre for Down's Syndrome);
         City of Birmingham Polytechnic   Cherrington, Derek, (Centre for
         9 Westbourne Road   Advanced Studies in Education,
         Edgbaston   Birmingham Polytechnic)
         Birmingham 15
         Tel: 021-454-3126

a) Effects of early developmental treatment and training on the Down's syndrome child.
b) The development of the Down's syndrome child from 3 to 5 years.

Background: Methods pioneered by Mr R. Brinkworth 1965 – 1983 for improving the
early development and intelligence of Down's syndrome children are being continuously
updated. Our aim is to enable the majority of Down's children to reach intelligence levels
which permit education in ESN(M) or normal schools. These results have been achieved
for many years now and we are investigating methods of improving on existing results.
Design: The main researcher is principal advisor and founder of Down's Children's
Association and the work has led since 1967 to a series of developmental programmes for
Down's children from birth to school age.
Currently we deal with 4500 children from 40 countries. Samples of experimental and
control children from 6 months to 18 years have been assessed on the Griffiths
developmental scales and the WISC and Reynell tests. Sample size is 1500 to date.
Methods: Parental intervention with professional advice involving intensive early
multisensory stimulation, detailed motor training from birth, pre-school education and
use of supplements of vitamins and minerals plus acetylcholine precursors with children
over 11 years.
Statistical results on samples (1965 to 1983) indicate rises in developmental quotient of 15
points for boys and 20 points for girls. Some 60 per cent of treated children can profit from
education in ESN(M) schools, while 1 per cent have been placed in normal infant, junior,
middle and secondary schools to date. Further analysis on full samples in progress.

Date of Research: a) November 1965 b) September 1983 – September 1987 (interim
reports annually).

Published Material: BRINKWORTH, R., and COLLINS, J.E. (1968). *Improving babies
with Down's Syndrome*, Belfast: RSMHC.
BRINKWORTH, R. (1973). 'Effects of early home training on the mongol infant'.
Mental Retardation and Behavioural Research. Ed: ADB Clark & A. Clark. London:
Churchill Livingstone.
BRINKWORTH, R. (1975). 'The unfinished child', *Royal Society of Health Journal*,
April.
BRINKWORTH, R. (1981). 'Early treatment and training for the child with Down's
syndrome', *Pontificia Academia Scientiarum*, R.V.M., Rome.
BRINKWORTH, R. (1983). 'The effects of early parental intervention on the child with
Down's syndrome'. *Collected Original Research in Education (CORE).* Ed: D. Cherring-
ton. Oxford: Carfax Publishers.
BRINKWORTH, R. (1984). *Down's Children Association Parent Guides: 1. 0 to 6 months;
2. 6 months to 5 years; 3. 2 years to 5 years.* London: DCA (revised edition).

KEYWORDS: *developmental programme; diet; Down's syndrome; pre-school*

1/011   Faculty of Education   Hunt, Elizabeth J., Mrs
              City of Birmingham Polytechnic   *Supervisor:* James, W.R.K.
              Westbourne Road
              Edgbaston
              Birmingham B15 3TN
              Tel: 021-454-5106

Written and oral responding in the education of handicapped children.

Background: This enquiry is part of a wider study of the role and potential for responding through oral, written and other modes by children undergoing special education.
The aim of the enquiry was to present the case that 'responding' was a vital component of classroom learning which teachers could exploit more effectively, and to illustrate the argument with evidence on the current state of these skills in special school classrooms.
Design: Childrens' responses in oral and written modes were examined with respect to quantity and to quality using criteria which enabled very low levels of performance to be identified and discussed in positive terms.
Size: 75 ESN(M) and 65 physically handicapped children.
Methods: Observations were carried out by teachers in their normal classroom setting while pursuing their usual lessons. The proportion of time devoted to teacher utterances and to children's responding were quantified with the support of detailed check-lists on classroom procedures.

Results: Results demonstrated wide variations in ability to respond within all class groups. There were indications that some children were not able to make constructed or coherent statements in any of the traditional modes. This carried implications that many children who may have ideas they wish to share will lack the means of expressing them. It was also clear that children who are the least able to benefit from verbally presented experiences and instruction tend to get more of it than children who can spend part of a lesson in expressive activity.
The case for systematic development of responding skills in all modalities was argued and the suggestion that alternative modes of making statements was a theme in urgent need of investigation.

Date of Research: January 1982–July 1983.

KEYWORDS: *responding skills; teaching approach; ESN(M) schools; physical handicap*

1/012   City of Birmingham Polytechnic   Stockdale, Shirley, Mrs
              Faculty of Education   *Supervisor:* James, W.R.K.
              Westbourne Road
              Edgbaston
              Birmingham B15 3TN
              Tel: 021-454-5106

Provision and uses of micro-technology in special education: an annual survey of the 'state of the art' in special schools in the West Midlands.

Background: The aim of the enquiry was to review the state of micro-technology and computer provision in special schools so that teachers might have access to information on schools which use particular computers and to facilitate exchange of working practices or software.
Design: The survey is to be repeated annually to monitor changes in provision and application of computer aided learning in all of the special schools in the West Midland Region.

Methods: A sample of 46 schools which provide special education for children with severe learning difficulty, physical handicap, visual impairment, hearing impairment and moderate learning difficulty participated in the sruvey. They supplied information through questionnaire and interview on microcomputer resources, staff experience, patterns of computer use, curriculum context and influences which have shaped these practices.

Results: Survey data of April 1983 indicated that this is a rapidly changing scene, with the 56 per cent of schools already in possession of computers rising to 86 per cent when firm orders for computers were taken into account. The most popular model was the BBC(B) with 43 per cent of provision, this rising to 53 per cent on completion of current orders.
Schools for physically handicapped children had the highest ratio of computers per school (3.6), while schools for children with moderate learning difficulty had 1.4 per school. Patterns of computer use indicated that the classroom was the most favoured location, and while they supported learning in areas of perceptual development, motor skills, communication, spelling etc., it was mathematics which predominated.
A wide range of peripheral equipment was found to be under development to simplify computer operation and provide access to CAL for the more severely disabled children.

Date of Research: January 1983–July 1983 (and annually thereafter).

KEYWORDS: *special school survey; microcomputer; software; computer equipment*

Birmingham University

1/013   Research Centre for the Education of   Tobin, Michael J., Dr
the Visually Handicapped
Department of Special Education
University of Birmingham
59 Selly Wick Road
Birmingham B29 7JE
Tel: 021-471-1303

Longitudinal investigation of cognitive development and educational achievement in blind and partially sighted children.

Background: This investigation, begun in 1973, aims to monitor aspects of the psychological and educational development of blind and partially sighted children attending special schools for the visually handicapped in England and Wales.
Size: The sample of 120 is estimated as constituting some 47 per cent of the age-group, the visual acuities of the children ranging upwards from nil to 4/36 plus (as measured on the Snellen chart).
Methods: The subjects are tested at least once every year by the researcher and his assistants. Among the major variables being measured are: print and braille reading; mathematics attainment; short-term memory; verbal and non-verbal reasoning; speed of information processing; various 'Piagetian' constructs; personality and self-concept. Degree of residual vision, cause of visual defect, age of onset and social class constitute some of the major independent variables.

Date of Research: September 1973–Ongoing.

Published Material: TOBIN, M.J. (1979). 'A longitudinal study of the blind and partially sighted children in special schools in England and Wales', *Insight*, **1**, 1, 11–14.

KEYWORDS: *visual impairment; longitudinal; attainment; cognition*

1/014   Department of Sociology   *Supervisor:* Lane, David
               University of Birmingham
               PO Box 363
               Birmingham B15 2TT

Current interdisciplinary bibliography on Down's syndrome.

Background: Bibliography covers medicine, genetics, psychology, education, law, social administration sociology.
Covers journal articles over three most recent years.
Design: English language sources.

Date of Research: Published annually.

Published Material: LANE, D. (1983). *Multidisciplinary Bibliography of Recent Research (1979–82) on Down's Syndrome.* London: Down's Children's Association.

KEYWORDS: bibliography; Down's syndrome

1/015   Research Centre for the Education of   Heritage, Raymond S.
               the Visually Handicapped   *Supervisor:* Tobin, M.J., Dr
               Department of Special Education
               University of Birmingham
               59 Selly Wick Road
               Birmingham B29 7JE
               Tel: 021-471-1301

Primary mathematics project.

Background: The aims of this project are to help experienced teachers with ideas and structures to embody in their work, and to produce a guide to the teaching of mathematics to visually handicapped pupils at the primary school level. The guide should be suitable for use by new recruits to this area of teaching.
Design: The principal way in which the work is being implemented is by teacher 'working parties', leading to the regular production of newsletters and preliminary background papers. These will form the basis of a final document/report embodying a mathematics syllabus and ground-plan that take account of the problems posed by severe visual impairment.

Date of Research: 1982–1985.

KEYWORDS: visual impairment, curriculum development; primary; mathematics

1/016   Department of Special Education   Richmond, Robin C.; Smith,
               Faculty of Education   Colin J.
               University of Birmingham   *Supervisor:* Gulliford, R., Prof.
               PO Box 363
               Birmingham B15 2TT

An evaluation of support and advice to ordinary schools for meeting the needs of children with learning difficulties.

Background: The Warnock report and the 1981 Act have stressed the importance of supporting ordinary schools to meet the needs of children with learning difficulties already in those schools. LEA peripatetic remedial services have traditionally filled this role and are likely to be the paradigm for future developments in special needs support services. This study is concerned with an LEA remedial education service and in particular the work of remedial advisory teachers.

Design: An 'illuminative evaluation' of the work of an LEA advisory and support service for special needs in the ordinary school. The study will be focussed on a group of children identified as experiencing learning difficulties by the LEA 7+ screening procedure.

Size: Phase 1: Project schools 11; Project children 60; Project class teachers 21; Project special needs advisory teachers 8.

Methods: Interview; questionnaire; case study; objective test results.

Date of Research: January 1984–1986.

KEYWORDS: *advisory teacher; learning difficulties; remedial service; support service*

1/017   Research Centre for the Education of   Tobin, M.J., Dr
               the Visually Handicapped
               Department of Special Education
               University of Birmingham
               59 Selly Wick Road
               Birmingham B29 7JE
               Tel: 021-471-1303

Microcomputer assisted learning for the blind and partially sighted.

Background: This project aims to assist in the development and implementation of microcomputer assisted learning in schools for the blind and partially sighted and in specialist units attached to 'ordinary' schools. (Software is also being developed that will be of use to teachers of newly-blinded adults who wish to learn braille.)

Design: Several working groups of teachers have been set up, and are being helped by the researcher to produce materials in the areas of visual perception training, the needs of the multi-handicapped blind, and mathematics. Newsletters and software documentation are being distributed to the schools, and short training courses are being mounted for teachers and peripatetic advisers.

Date of Research: September 1983–August 1986.

KEYWORDS: computer assisted learning; visual impairment; microcomputer; Braille; software; adult; visual perception; mathematics

Bradford University

1/018   Department of Education   McCree Edbury, J., Mrs
               University of Bradford   *Supervisor:* Rees, Olav, Dr
               Bradford
               West Yorkshire BD7 1DP

The development of a language programme for slow learning children.

Background: To explore the language teaching of slow learning children at the adolescent stage in special schools and comprehensive schools.

Design: An empirical study was conducted in which a structured language programme was designed, using a core vocabulary of abstract words taken from a 19,000 word count of nouns and verbs used in radio and television newscasts. The programme was tested on four groups of children, aged 12–14 years, with a verbal reasoning IQ in the range 60–80, two groups acting as experimental groups and two as controls, over a period of six months.

Results: The provision of a structured language programme, containing extending contexts, is likely to be much more effective in improving the slow learning child's understanding of abstract words.

Date of Research: January 1980–May 1983.

KEYWORDS: language; slow learner; adolescence; secondary

1/019   School of Psychology   Muldoon, John
               University of Bradford   *Supervisor:* Riseborough, M., Dr
               Great Horton Road
               Bradford
               West Yorkshire

The social psychology of parental involvement in the education of children with special needs.

Background: The Warnock Report and the subsequent Education Act (1981) have placed great emphasis on the need for parental involvement in the education of children with special needs. Accounts of parents' dissatisfaction with their opportunities for collaboration with professionals has been widely reported, though, and this research is concerned with the effect of aspects of parent/teacher interactions in this phenomenon. Within the framework of symbolic interactionism, this study critically examines the role of positivistic paradigms in shaping the social construction of professional assumptions with regard to the problems and needs which parents encounter in adjusting to children with special needs. Goffman's notion of 'information control' in response to the process of stigmatization is put forward as an explanation of problematic aspects of parent/teacher interaction; and this is placed in contrast to the positivistic accounts referred to above.

Design: (1) Parent interviews to detect parental expectations of involvement with schools, and their estimation of current practice.

(2) Teacher interviews to detect teachers' expectations of parental involvement; assumptions with regard to 'causes' of parents' problems.

(3) Participation observation of one parent self-help group.

Methods: Interview; participation observation.

Date of Research: January 1983–Ongoing.

KEYWORDS: parental involvement; symbolic interactionism

Brighton Polytechnic

1/020   Chelsea School of Human Movement   Lawton, Shelagh, Ms
         Brighton Polytechnic   *Supervisor:* Allen, John, Dr (Dept
         Gaudick Road   of Community Studies, Brighton
         Eastbourne   Polytechnic); Henderson, Sheila,
         Tel: 0323-21400 ext. 275   Dr (Dept of Child Development,
                                             London University Institute of
                                             Education); Mc C. Smith, Joy,
                                             Miss (Chelsea School of Human
                                             Movement, Brighton Polytechnic)

Motor control in Down's syndrome children.

Background: To identify the nature of the specific motor deficit experienced by Down's syndrome children by analysis of both the perceptual and motor components of skilled behaviour; interpret findings in the context of theories and models of normal motor performance; and determine whether this subgroup of handicapped children have particular problems affecting specifically the temporal and/or spatial aspects of controlled motor behaviour.

Design: Experimentation will initially examine the use of temporal anticipation in Down's syndrome and control subjects. Further research will examine several other factors which may account for their apparent slower performance, such as hypotonia, extraneous muscular activity or delay in central decision-making processes.

Size: The majority of experimentation will involve the assessment of at least 30 Down's syndrome children (7–14 years) matched with other mentally handicapped children of the same MA and CA and with normal children of similar MAs.

Methods: Initial experimentation will involve the use of a coincident timing task, requiring either a simple manual or vocal response to assess the subject's ability to use temporal anticipation.

Date of Research: August 1983–August 1986.

KEYWORDS: Down's syndrome; spatial ability; motor control; temporal anticipation

---

1/0121   Faculty of Education Studies   Parkyn, Leonard A.
         Brighton Polytechnic   *Supervisors:* Modgil, Sohan, Dr;
         Falmer   Cross, G.R., Dr (Faculty of
         Brighton   Education, King's College)
         East Sussex
         Tel: 0273-606622

An investigation into the patterning of social maturity in relation to cognitive development among ESN children.

Background: To investigate the patterning of social maturity in relation to cognitive development among ESN children.

Design: The study will examine the following hypotheses:

1. That ESN children will tend to possess a negative disproportionate social development when related to their intellectual functioning level as measured by intelligence tests.

2. That ESN children are socially immature in relation to their chronological age.

3. That there would be no significant differences in social maturity between the pre-operational ESN group and the operational ESN group.

4. That there would be significant differences in social maturity between the 'normal' operational group and the ESN operational group.
Size: N = 150 children with chronological age approximately from 7 to 18 years, with equal numbers of males and females. The children will be selected from ESN school.
Methods: Following an initial pilot investigation, ESN subjects will be grouped in accordance with the Piagetian developmental continuum ranging from pre-operational, transitional and fully concrete operational. The final grouping will depend on the results of the pilot investigation: modifications may be deemed necessary. The differing Piagetian levels will be established through the administration of Piagetian tests.

Date of Research: September 1983–July 1986.

KEYWORDS: *cognitive development; maturation; Piaget; social maturity; ESN*

Bristol Polytechnic

1/022   Department of Education   Buckland, Marie, Mrs
               Bristol Polytechnic   *Supervisors:* Croll, Paul; Jones,
               Redland Hill   Ken
               Redland
               Bristol BS6 6UZ
               Tel: 0272-741251

The use of logo with children who have special educational needs and the effect it has on their level of functioning.

Background: For two terms older children with learning difficulties used OK logo and a floor turtle. Having analysed the results of this trial, the researcher's aim was to develop a more suitable form of logo for younger less able children and to study its effect on their level of functioning.
Design: An action research method of development of turtling in Glevum was adopted; there are seven carefully graded programs using a BBC microcomputer, a floor turtle and a concept keyboard.
Size: Since October 1983, the turtle program has been used by most of the children in the school – 100 children within the age range 6–15 years.
Methods: The researcher worked initially with small groups of children and later, after work sessions, observations and interviews with class teachers, the turtle program has been developed and used as a class activity under the direction of the individual class teacher.

Date of Research: April 1983–Ongoing.

KEYWORDS: *logo; microcomputer*

1/023   Bristol Polytechnic   Davidson, R.E.B., Mrs
               Faculty of Education & Community
               Studies
               Redland Hill
               Bristol B56 6UZ
               Tel: 0272-741251 ext.51

Interaction in classrooms for children with severe learning difficulties.

Background: The present study, in examining aspects of teacher–child interaction in two different situations (an individual 1:1 setting, and a group music session), will identify some teacher interactive strategies in five non-verbal and one verbal categories.
Design: Small-scale teachers' development group (four teachers). To produce some information on a very unresearched area in the teaching of severely mentally handicapped children – their classroom interaction.
Size: Approximately 30 children in four classes.
Methods: Video recording, analysis of coding categories. Comparison. Illuminative rather than statistics-based, although some basic statistics may be used where appropriate.

Date of Research: 1981/82–Due Autumn 1984.

KEYWORDS: interaction; severe learning difficulties

1/024   Faculty of Education and   Jones, Ken; Kirby, Maggie, Mrs
               Community Studies
               Bristol Polytechnic
               Redland Hill
               Bristol BS6 6UZ
               Tel: 0272-741251

Sherborne and Movement.

Background: Bristol Polytechnic sought funding for a 1-year project to allow an evaluation of Mrs Sherborne's work in order that her approach could be documented and continued after she ceases to practice.
Design: A descriptive study of the application of Veronica Sherborne's approach to the teaching of Movement in Bristol Polytechnic Department of Education, with reference both to initial training and in-service work.
Size: Questionnaires were sent to 359 teachers, including past students of Bristol Polytechnic. The work of twelve postgraduate students was followed throughout the year 1982/83.
Methods: Questionnaire to teachers; questionnaire to postgraduate students; participational observation; tape-recorded interviews; video-tapes.

Results: Mrs Sherborne's approach to the teaching of Movement is enthusiastically received by those who encounter it but it would appear that for some people a more theoretical input would be welcome.

Date of Research: October 1982–March 1984.

KEYWORDS: movement education; teacher training; Sherborne

1/025   Faculty of Education and   Davidson, R.E.B., Mrs
               Community Studies   *Supervisors:* Kyle, J., Dr
               Bristol Polytechnic   (University of Bristol School of
               Redland Hill   Education)
               Bristol BS6 6UZ
               Tel: 0272-741251 ext. 51

The use of rebuses in the teaching of reading to children with severe learning difficulties.

Background: Children with severe learning difficulties are taught reading as part of their curriculum in special schools. Reading in these schools is taught by a number of methods, and with a variety of materials.

An increasingly popular way of developing reading skills, whether as part of a reading programme, or for the development of general communication skills, is through the use of rebus symbols, or other mediated systems. The research described in this study investigated the use of an augmented reading scheme especially designed for the purpose: pictographic rebuses allied with words in traditional orthography.

Design: Intervention programme: seven schools; 15 teachers; 30 children. Use of specially designed booklets. Six months.

Size: See above. Thirty children were in day special schools (7 schools). Mixed handicaps (Down's syndrome, cerebral palsy, non-specific).

Methods: Before and post testing + intervention period.

Results: Seventeen out of 30 learned to read words but, as can be seen from the short report attached, there were complexities in the results – the implications being that teacher attitudes/expectations were very influential. Further study needed of this.

Date of Research: October 1979–January 1984.

KEYWORDS: *rebus; reading; severe learning difficulties; teacher attitude; pictorial symbol*

1/026   Department of Education   Withers, Robert, Dr
              Bristol Polytechnic
              Redland Hill
              Redland
              Bristol BS6 6UZ
              Tel: 0272-741251

The philosophy of special education.

Background: The research seeks to provide a philosophy for special education and hence to extend the scope of philosophical investigation in the philosophy of education and mind. It seeks to establish a justification for the principle of integration and examines central concepts in our understanding of persons. The meaning of 'special education' is explored by means of a consideration of these issues and concepts.

Design: The investigation and underlying argument is sustained through discussion of interrelated issues.

Methods: Philosophical.

Date of Research: September 1982–A book will result – to be completed by September 1985.

Published Material: WITHERS, R.A. (1983). 'Mary Warnock's "Doctrine of compassion" as a justification of special education', *Educational Review*, **35**, 3, 219–24.

KEYWORDS: *philosophy; conceptual analysis; ethics; integration*

British Association for Early Childhood Education

1/027   BAECE   Grubb, Jane, Dr
          Montgomery Hall
          Kennington Oval
          London SE11 5SW

British Association for Early Childhood Education (BAECE) survey of handicapped children in ordinary schools 1981–82.

Background: Survey was made to assess the real situation, at a time when no information was available.
Design: BAECE has members throughout the UK; all members were circulated with a questionnaire; this was carried out in late 1981 and returns were analysed in 1982/3.
Size: Total responses 177 with a wide geographical spread. From primary and middle schools 170 (comprehensives = 7). (Comprehensives were omitted from the analysis.)
Methods: Straightforward tabulated form.

Results: It appears that ordinary schools accept children with various sensory, physical, emotional and medical conditions, all likely to result in learning difficulties. At least 13 per cent of the survey schools had over 20 per cent of such children and in some, especially nursery schools, this was higher.
A list of recommendations was included.

Date of Research: October 1981–October 1984.

KEYWORDS: incidence of handicap; epidemiology

Brunel University

1/028   Department of Education   Wilkinson, John
          Brunel University   *Supervisor:* Barry, Susie, Dr
          Uxbridge
          Middlesex UB8 3PH
          Tel: 0895-37188

Teaching non-verbal social skills to adolescent special needs students in a college of FE.

Background: To teach special needs students on an FE course improved non-verbal social skills.
Design: Pretest of social skills, a set teaching programme, and retest. Total teaching period one year.
Size: Experimental group (taught) 8 students. Control groups (not taught) 8 in schools, 12 in adult training centre.
Methods: 1) Test is a self-adapted scale for social skills completed by staff. 2) Teaching is college-based lesson and role play using video.

Date of Research: September 1982–Ongoing.

KEYWORDS: social skills; adolescence; further education

Calderdale Education Department

1/029   ALSS   Cawley, Norman
              Calderdale Education Department   *Supervisors:* Clayton, B. (Maths
              Northgate House   Adviser, Calderdale); Cawley, N.
              Halifax   (Head, Assessment & Learning
              W. Yorks   Support, Calderdale)
              Tel: 0422-57257

Graded/Diagnostic Maths Test: secondary low attainers (based on Cockroft Foundation List).

Background: Assessment of lower attaining pupils at the early secondary stage, in concepts based on the Cockroft 'Foundation List' of Mathematical Abilities: *Mathematics Counts* (HMSO, 1983).
Design: Monitoring in up to 12 local authority secondary schools.
Methods: Teacher/pupil evaluation.

Date of Research: July 1983–July 1985.

KEYWORDS: *mathematics; assessment; secondary; low attainer*

Cambridge Institute of Education

1/030   Cambridgeshire Institute of   Child, John (Cambridge Institute);
              Education   Foster, G. (Inspector for Special
              Shaftesbury Road   Education, Cambridge)
              Cambridge CB2 2BX
              Tel: 0223-69631

Three joint LEA/Cambridge Institute Teacher Fellowships: (1) Developments since 1981 Act. (2) Curriculum for special educational needs in the comprehensive school. (3) INSET needs in the primary school.

Background: To examine LEA practice regarding aspects of special needs provision. Cambridgeshire LEA offered three secondments to be held as teacher fellowships at the Cambridge Institute of Education during the autumn term 1984.
Design: The studies are being conducted within Cambridgeshire and cover three topics: (i) the response of schools to the Education Act 1981 relating to children with special educational needs; (ii) balance in the comprehensive school curriculum: 14–16-year-olds with special educational needs; (iii) meeting special educational needs in the primary school: the role of the named teacher.

Date of Research: All September 1984 to January 1985 – possibility of 1 term extension.

KEYWORDS: *Education Act 1981; primary; secondary; named teacher; curriculum development; in-service education*

Cambridge University

1/031   Department of Education   Bruce, D.J., Dr; Wattles, Beryl,
          University of Cambridge   Mrs
          17 Trumpington Street   *Supervisors:* Zangwill, O.L., Prof.
          Cambridge CB2 1PT   (retired); Bruce, D.J., Dr
          Tel: 0223-64111

A follow-up study of backwardness in reading.

Background: Case records of children referred to the London Word-Blind Centre (1964–72) were placed in 1979 in the care of the Cambridge Specific Learning Disabilities Group for the purposes of follow-up research. The first investigation had as its principal aims: (1) Assessment of present competence in reading and spelling; (2) Delineation of educational history, with particular reference to areas of difficulty; (3) Information regarding remedial help received; (4) Information regarding occupational experience and strategies evolved for coping with associated difficulties.
Design: The research is seen as 'open-ended' since the case-record material is rich in pointers to useful investigation. Current planned projects include: (1) Comparison of remedial methods used at WBC (and effects) with other remedial schemes and systems; (2) Systematic analysis of job satisfaction and barriers to advancement; (3) Further study of coping strategies, with particular reference to memory difficulties.
Size: In the first investigation, 68 men and seven women ranging in age from 18.2 to 30.4, with a mean of 23.3 years.
Methods: Semi-structured interview procedure. Formal and informal tests, including Schonell graded word spelling (form B), Neale anlaysis of reading ability (form A), digit-span, sentence learning, serial subtraction, and verbal fluency.

Results: (1) Difficulties *re* remedial help and examination concessions; (2) Substantial improvement in oral reading skill, related to amount of remedial teaching; (3) Continuing problem with spelling; improvement apparently related to specific WBC teaching; (4) Downward shift in occupational status, with recourse to employment making only a light demand on verbal skills; (5) Sharp contrasts in educational success between traditional arts subjects and mathematical/scientific/technical subjects; (6) Sensitivity to disability revealed in coping strategies.

Date of Research: 1980–July 1982 (first investigation). Research continuing.

Published Material: BRUCE, D.J. (1983). 'Coping with dyslexia', *Cambridge Journal of Education*, **13,** 3, 16–22.

KEYWORDS: reading; specific learning disabilities; assessment; dyslexia

Centre for Advancement of Mathematical Education in Technology

1/032   CAMET   Green, David R., Dr
          University of Technology
          Loughborough LE11 3TU
          Tel: 0509-263171 ext. 5146

Microcomputers for concepts of statistics and mathematics (MICROCOSM).

Background: The aim is to produce software for special schools (physically handicapped and ESN) to introduce fundamental mathematical concepts (appropriate to infant level) as found in Piaget's book *The Child's Conception of Number*.
Design: A suite of about ten programs have been designed and tried out in special schools. Pupil reaction has been monitored and modifications made. The programs use the BBC microcomputer and concept keyboard for inputs.
Size: Two principal schools were used but about 12 others have evaluated the material with their own pupils.
Methods: A rigorous research style has not been possible. Feedback has therefore come from teachers observing pupils and commenting on the programs and reporting on the usefulness of the materials.

Results: No firm conclusions are yet available. The evidence to date shows that children are strongly motivated to use the computer to perform simple mathematical tasks such as making one-to-one correspondences of objects, ordering objects etc, using screen images.

Date of Research: September 1983–December 1984.

Published Material: GREEN, D.R. and CAHILL, S. (1984). *Introducing Fundamental Mathematical Concepts to Handicapped Pupils.* Proceedings of International Conference on 'The Computer as an Aid for Those with Special Needs', Sheffield City Polytechnic, pp. 17–25.
GREEN, D.R., LEWIS, P.E. and CAHILL, S. (1984). *The Use of a Microcomputer with Concept Keyboard to Provide Elementary Number Concept Experiences for Handicapped Children.* Proceedings of 'Micros in Education' Conference, Loughborough University.

KEYWORDS: mathematics; Piaget; microcomputer; software; physical handicap; ESN

Chelmer Institute of Higher Education

1/033   Educational Research Centre   Best, Ronald
             Chelmer Institute of Higher
             Education
             Sawyers Hall Lane
             Brentwood
             Essex BM5 9BT
             Tel: 0277-216971

An investigation of remedial education in the comprehensive school.

Background: Building on by-products of an earlier (SSRC funded) project on pastoral care, this project aims to compare and contrast the organization and philosophy of remedial provision in two 11–16 comprehensive schools.
Design: This project is the subject of M. Phil/PhD registration at the University of East Anglia and began in October 1981. The first (completed) stage was a review of the literature and formulation of a tentative theory of teacher perspectives on 'remediality'. The second phase (in progress) involved interview and observation in two contrasting 11–16 comprehensives. A hundred or so interviews/observations have been recorded to date and a preliminary processing of the data (using R. Winter's model of 'dilemma analysis') has been undertaken. Data-collection will be completed by July 1984, and the analysis/report concluded by July 1985.

Date of Research: October 1981–July 1985.

KEYWORDS: remedial education; secondary; teacher perspective

Child Guidance Centre

1/034   Child Guidance Centre   Narrough, Stephen Andrew
          Old School House   *Supervisors:* Daly, G. (Internal
          23 Main Street   supervisor; The OU Northern
          Lumphinnans   Reg., Newcastle); Quinault, F., Dr
          Fife KY4 9HQ   (External supervisor; Dept. of
          Tel: 0383-512869   Psychology, St. Andrews
                                            University)

A longitudinal evaluation of an early screening procedure (which is developmentally oriented and school based) and the intervention which follows it.

Background: Principal aim – long-term evaluation of the predictive accuracy of a 3-tier screening procedure – school-based with observation by teachers using a developmentally oriented checklist as first stage. Subsidiary aim – some comment on effectiveness of follow up recommendations coming from the accompanying handbook.

Design: Checklist/screening completed during first year of compulsory education: attempting to complete the evaluation of system and provide (in conjunction with other local authority staff) necessary back-up services and materials.

Size: Total sample will be in excess of 2000 over key four years 1978–82; boys and girls from representative sample of primary schools in West Fife. Subsequently (1983 to present) a broader sample over all of Fife.

Methods: Comparison of checklist results with further standardized testing of whole group and individuals. No formal control group but reference to performances of same and similar schools before screening started in terms of group/individual testing and referral patterns to child guidance/special education. Allowances being considered for staff and catchment area changes and influence of other factors, e.g. nursery education.

Results: Preliminary results: the scheme seems to be practicable and quite well received by teachers. It appears to err on the side of false positives but as the checklist predicts 'likely risk of educational difficulty' this is to be accepted.

Date of Research: Current phase: February 1982 (original phase: September 1977) – Estimated Autumn 1986 (but could be as late as January 1990).

Published Material: NARBROUGH, S.A. (1980). Educational screening at Primary One. Unpublished dissertation to the BPS for the Dip. Dev. & Ed. Psych.

KEYWORDS: screening; longitudinal; checklist

Christ Church College, Canterbury

1/035   Psychology Department   Agnew, Nan, Ms
          Christ Church College   *Supervisor:* Povey, R.M., Dr
          Canterbury
          Kent CT1 1QU
          Tel: 0227-65548

Teaching chess to physically handicapped pupils.

Background: To examine the feasibility of teaching chess to physically handicapped pupils.

Design: The project took place in an all-age (3–18) school for physically handicapped pupils in London.

Size: Fifteen children were involved between the ages of seven and 13 years and suffering from a variety of handicaps including cerebral palsy, muscular dystrophy and spina bifida.

Methods: Pupils were taught the rudimentary skills of chess within the context of the normal school timetable by one of the authors (NA) using an approach she had designed herself (the Initial Chess Teaching Method).

Results: It is concluded that the method offers a useful teaching approach for pupils in the 7–13 age group and the project lends support to the view that chess could well take its place as a useful component of the school curriculum whether in mainstream or special education.

Date of Research: April 1982–October 1983.

Published Material: AGNEW, N. and POVEY, R. (1984). 'Chess for the physically handicapped', *Special Education: Forward Trends*, **11**, 3, 371.
AGNEW, N. (1984). *The Initial Chess Teaching Method.* The Spastic Society, 16 Fitzroy Square, London W1P 5HQ.

KEYWORDS: *chess; physical handicap*

1/036   Psychology Department   Manley, Ruth, Miss
           Christ Church College   *Supervisor:* Povey, R.M., Dr
           Canterbury
           Kent CT1 1QU
           Tel: 0227-65548

The use of 'Breakthrough to Literacy' with mentally handicapped adults.

Background: The paper reports the use of the Breakthrough to Literacy scheme with five mentally handicapped adults at a Social Education Centre. The subjects were aged between 18 and 48 years.
It is concluded that a modified version of the scheme has considerable potential for use with mentally handicapped adults.

Date of Research: April 1982–June 1983.

Published Material: MANLEY, R. and POVEY, R. (1985). '"Breakthrough to Literacy": its use with adults who are mentally handicapped'. *Mental Handicap*, **13**, March, pp. 20–1.

KEYWORDS: *reading; mental retardation; mentally handicapped adults; special education; teaching method*

Communication Aids for Learners in Lothian Centre

1/037   CALL Centre   Odor, J.P.
           Annex   *Supervisor:* Entwhistle, N.J., Prof.,
           4 Buccleuch Place   and Odor, J.P. (Education Dept.,
           Edinburgh   Godfrey Thomson Unit)
           Tel: 031-667-1438
                031-667-1011 ext. 6713

Communication aids for learners in Lothian.

Background: To investigate the potential uses of new microelectronic communication aids in the context of conventional and microcomputer-based learning.
Design: (i) Intensive case studies of the communication needs of handicapped learners, including provision of the appropriate aid. (ii) Development of new communication systems and components.
Size: For the case studies, five individuals with different disabilities but having in common a significant communication handicap.
Methods: For the case studies, each individual's needs are assessed and a cooperative programme of work developed with parents, teachers, therapists or employers as appropriate. This programme will be supported with computer-based and other technical assistance and with continuing advice and instruction. For the development work, a wide range of devices and interfaces is being developed to suit different types and degrees of disability.

Date of Research: May 1983–May 1985.

Published Material: NISBET, P. *Universal Optoisolated Input Adaptor Unit*, Edinburgh: CALL Centre.

ODOR, J.P. Some Components of a Hard Communication Technology. Edinburgh: CALL Centre.
CALL CENTRE (1983). *An Introduction to the CALL (Communication Aids for Learners in Lothian) Centre Project*. University of Edinburgh.

KEYWORDS: computer assisted learning; communication aid; microcomputer

Crewe and Alsager College of Higher Education

1/038   Department of Special Education   Alston, Jean
              Crewe and Alsager College of Higher
              Education
              Crewe
              Cheshire CW1 1DU
              Tel: 0270-583661

An examination of the developmental, cognitive and instructional aspects of handwriting, with special reference to pupils in Cheshire primary schools.

Background: Data collected from a representative sample of Cheshire primary school children began in January 1981 when writing samples were collected from a 7 + cohort. The initial aim was to standardize a handwriting checklist. Subsequently, the 7 + children have been asked to complete handwriting samples as they have progressed through their primary schools.
Design: The 7 + handwriting samples were employed in the examination of reliability and validity of the handwriting checklist. The handwriting of the same group of children has been monitored annually during the academic years 1981/2, 1982/3 and 1983/4.
Pupils showing handwriting problems in their third junior school year are identified; an analysis of their problems will be pursued and appropriate remedial programmes will be constructed.
Size: Seventeen Cheshire schools were identified as being representative of the county in terms of socio-economic distribution, school size and urban-rural location. The sample consisted of approximately 500 children in each year.

Methods: On two sequential years, five teachers were employed to rate handwriting samples on a seven-point scale and to mark them on a handwriting checklist using a prescribed marking system.

Results: The handwriting checklist, published in 1981, is a reliable and valid measure which could be used in quantitative research. An item analysis identified 13 items as contributing to *legibility* in handwriting as it is understood by teachers.
It is possible to identify normative data in handwriting. Normative samples, ranging from 'very poor' to 'very good' on a seven point scale, are available for Cheshire children aged 7 +, 8 + and 9 + years of age.

Date of Research: September 1981–June 1986.

Published Material: ALSTON, J. (1981). *Handwriting Checklist.* Wisbech: Learning Development Aids.
ALSTON, J. (1983a). 'Handwriting and legibility: a model for the selection of normative writing samples', *Remedial Education*, February.
ALSTON, J. (1983b). 'A legibility index: can handwriting be measured?' *Educational Review*, Autumn.
ALSTON, J. and TAYLOR, J. (1984). *The Handwriting File.* Wisbech: Learning Development Aids.

KEYWORDS: handwriting; checklist; primary; screening; legibility

Derbyshire County Educational Psychology Service

1/039   Derbyshire County Educational   Goulding, S., Mrs
             Psychology Service
             Area Education Office
             The Crescent
             Buxton
             Derbyshire
             Tel: 0298-6121

A system to deliver individual learning programmes to slow learning children in a range of normal and special educational settings – a pilot study.

Background: To examine the feasibility of a Portage-style system for delivering and supporting individual learning programmes in schools across an area of a local education authority.
Size: Presently involving about 120 children selected from 150 school settings.
Methods: Datapac materials and related Direct Instruction and Precision Teaching materials.

Results: Not yet available.

Date of Research: November 1982–late 1984.

Published Material: BOOTH, S. and JEWEL, T. (1982). 'Programmes for slow learners', *AEP Journal*, **6,** 2.
MILLER, A., BOOTH, S., JEWEL, T. and ROBSON, D. (in press). 'A system for delivering educational programmes to slow learners'. *AEP Journal.*

KEYWORDS: direct instruction; precision teaching; Portage; support service

Dorset Institute of Higher Education

1/040   Department of Nursing and Social   Norris, David
           Studies
           Dorset Institute of Higher Education
           Wallisdown Road
           Poole
           Dorset BH12 5BB
           Tel: 0202-524111

The significance of the adult in the use of language by severely retarded children.

Background: Project originally constructed to test efficacy of a device designed to promote social cooperation in severely retarded children. Due to persistent mechanical failure, project modified to restrict its scope to examining the extent to which children communicate among themselves and to the teacher.

Design: Project studies extent of child/child contact and language, child-initiated child/adult contact and language. Seeks to examine differences in Down's/non Down's children and sex differences. Differences in free play and sedentary lessons.

Size: 6 boys, 4 girls CA 5–8 IQ 20–35.

Methods: Observation and written record.

Date of Research: January 1983–March 1985.

KEYWORDS: language; play; severe learning difficulties; Down's syndrome; primary; communication

Dundee University

1/041   School of Social Administration   Buist, Maureen, Ms
           University of Dundee
           Dundee

The role of guidance and remedial teachers in the assistance of vulnerable children.

Background: How does school respond to the demands of socially disadvantaged children? What are the tasks of guidance teachers? Do they differ in schools serving disadvantaged areas? How accurate were the predictions of primary teachers that a proportion of the children would fail as a consequence of behaviour and/or learning difficulties?

Size: Four schools, 19 guidance teachers, four remedial teachers provide qualitative information. 665 pupils – qualitative information.

Methods: Semi-structured interviews with teachers. These were tape recorded and transcribed. In addition, information was collected on aspects of the children in S3 or S4 in each of the schools and recorded in the computer (remedial provision during school career, disciplinary incidents, O-grades studied, handicaps etc.).

Results: Schools serving disadvantaged areas have far greater demands made on them in comparison with their more fortunate colleagues yet they rarely are compensated for this by extra guidance or remedial staff. There appears to be a need for training in teaching skills for social education classes to maximize opportunities therefore assisting pupils. There is need for improvements in interprofessional work particularly with social workers.

Date of Research: April 1983–May 1984.

Published Material: None yet except report to SED.

KEYWORDS: guidance teacher; remedial service; learning difficulties; support service; social education; in-service education

Dunfermline College of Physical Education

1/042   Department of Movement and   Murdoch, Elizabeth B., Miss
               Rehabilitation
               Dunfermline College of Physical
               Education
               Cramond Road North
               Edinburgh EH4 6JD
               Tel: 031-336-6001

An investigation into diagnosis of and possible remedial measures for minimal motor impairment in school children.

Background: The project is a collaborative one involving the assessment unit of the Royal Hospital for Sick Children in Glasgow, and Dunfermline College of Physical Education. There are three main aims: (1) Review of all published relevant material; (2) Specific appraisal of existing forms of assessment (tests and programmes); (3) Design and construction of a form of assessment coupled with a remedial programme suitable for children in Scottish schools.
Size: Focus is children who have a degree of motor impairment, insufficiently severe to qualify for medical treatment and follow-up but which nevertheless affects their physical performance and learning at school.
Methods: In preparation; videotape a likely medium.

Date of Research: October 1981–December 1985.

KEYWORDS: physical education; assessment; remedial provision; motor impairment

East Park School, Glasgow

1/043   East Park School   Wilson, Elizabeth, Miss
               Maryhill
               Glasgow

The use of soft play equipment with multiply handicapped children.

Background: 'Totally soft play environment' is new in many schools for the physically handicapped child; it is very expensive and therefore must be proved worthwhile for all children. My particular aim was to use it for the multiply handicapped child and record their reaction and response.

Date of Research: October 1983.

KEYWORDS: soft play equipment; physical handicap; mutiple handicap

Edinburgh University

1/044   Department of Education   Thomson, George O.B., Dr;
         University of Edinburgh   Buultjens; Marianna, Mrs; Budge,
         10 Buccleuch Place   Alexander
         Edinburgh

Meeting the special educational needs of the visually handicapped – the process of decision making.

Background: Following on the Education (Scotland) Act 1981, the study proposes to investigate in detail how education authorities throughout Scotland are implementing policy decisions concerning the visually handicapped in respect of that element in the Act concerned with parental choice. It is likely that this element of the Act will contribute to an increasing trend towards 'integration' for the individual pupil.

Design: The investigation should identify issues for policy implementation, service delivery and the evaluation of these services that might apply to other handicapped groups.

Methods: The study will use questionnaire and interview techniques to derive data from policy makers, those who implement policy and the handicapped group.

Date of Research: September 1984–August 1985.

KEYWORDS: visual impairment; integration; Education Act 1981; policy

Edington Senior School, Shapwick

1/045   Edington Senior School   Chinn, S.J., Dr
         Shapwick Manor
         Shapwick
         nr. Bridgewater
         Somerset TA7 9NJ

Self-voice echo techniques for basic fact learning with dyslexia.

Background: The Arrow tape machine (C. Lane) may provide an effective extra learning method for basic facts for learning disabled pupils.

Design: Five methods for learning times tables were compared.

Size: 25 learning disabled pupils, aged 13–17, all scoring 3/15 or below on times tables facts 6×7 to 9×9.

Methods: Five pupils were allocated to each consecutive method and tutored/supervised for 10-minute sessions for five consecutive days. They were retested on the 15 facts after 24 hours, 7 days and 4 weeks. Each pupil was tested with the Koppitz Visual, Aural Draft Span Test to determine their area of weakness in memory.

Results: Data now complete and awaiting analysis. Initial impressions suggest that it is the pupil's *own* voice which is crucial.

Date of Research: September 1983–Autumn 1984.

KEYWORDS: dyslexia; learning disabled; self-voice technique

Glasgow University

1/046   Department of Education   Dunn, William R.
         University of Glasgow
         Glasgow G12 8QQ
         Tel: 041-339-8855

The education of hearing impaired children with additional handicaps.

Background: The project is a collaborative one involving Glasgow University, Strath-clyde Regional Council and the Greater Glasgow Health Board. It is concernd with the educational needs of hearing impaired children who have additional handicaps.
Design: The project has two facets: (1) The development of assessment techniques for the multi-handicapped deaf which are relevant to teaching strategies; and (2) The development of a framework in which information from the various disciplines can be brought together in such a way that the educational implications are clarified.
Size: Variable. Researchers will supply further information.
Methods: Survey and analysis (teachers and pupils) viedeo for teaching purposes.

Date of Research: September 1981–August 1984.

Published Material: BRYSON, E. and DUNN, W. R. (1982a). Survey of Views of Teachers of the Deaf Concerning Hearing-impaired Children with Additional Handicaps. Glasgow University
BRYSON, E. and DUNN, W.R. (1982b). Survey of Views about Sensory Impairments in Schools for Severely and Profoundly Mentally Handicapped Children. Glasgow University.
BRYSON, E., MASSEY, A. and DUNN, W.R. (1982). Investigation into Children Reported as Deaf and Blind in Schools for the Profoundly Mentally Handicapped. Glasgow University.

KEYWORDS: hearing impairment; multiple handicap; deaf/blind; survey; sensory impairment; assessment; multidisciplinary

1/047   Department of Education   McCormack, Andrina E., Ms
         University of Glasgow   *Supervisor:* Wilkinson, J.E.
         Glasgow G12 8QQ
         Tel: 041-339-8855

Language Fluency Project.

Background: The topic of LFP is socialized language and mentally handicapped children. The aim of LFP was to investigate the elements of socialized language, to develop group and individual assessment mechanisms for use with class groups in special schools and units, and to develop a training programme to encourage socialized language facility in mentally handicapped children and slow learners.
Design: LFP was designed in phases.
Phase 1: Investigation of the effects of discussion sessions on the socialized/open-ended language of a group of mentally handicapped girls.
Phase 2: Development of classroom analysis system.
Phase 3: Development of socialized profile.
Phase 4: Development of training programme.
Phase 5: Survey of teachers' attitude to language curricula.
Size: Four schools were involved in piloting and retesting the training programme.

Methods: Flanders Interaction Analysis System; item discrimination; factor analysis; questionnaire; interview schedule; report back from participants.

Results: Mentally handicapped adolescents showed a behaviour improvement in their use of socialized language, which should receive greater emphasis in the special education setting, in order to encourage like skills and independence more effectively, and to promote integration of mentally handicapped teenagers on leaving school.

Date of Research: August 1977–January 1985.

KEYWORDS: Mental handicap; ESN(M); Communication; Language

Hertfordshire College of Higher Education

1/048   Hertfordshire College of Higher   Kernohan, H.
              Education
              Wall Hall
              Aldenham
              Watford
              Tel: 09276-2511

Visual memory processes in deaf and normal-hearing children.

Design: This study investigated the short-term visual memory for simultaneously presented stimuli, arranged in composite picture form, in two age-groups of profoundly hearing-impaired primary age children, by comparing it with control groups of normal hearing children.

Size: The ages of the subjects were approximately six years and ten years and there were 18 subjects in each group. All the hearing-impaired subjects are taught using oral methods which are supplemented by cued speech or manual signs.

Methods: Presentation time (five seconds or 15 seconds) and retention interval (immediate recall or recall after 30 seconds) were varied, in a fixed order, across low and high levels of complexity of task for each of the four experimental groups.

Results: The results indicated that the ten-year-old hearing-impaired subjects are equal to their normal hearing peers for both levels of complexity of task but that the six-year-old normal hearing subjects are superior to the hearing-impaired six-year-olds at both levels of complexity ($p < .01$). The results confirm an increase in memory with age for the hearing-impaired and control subjects ($p < .001$). Complexity of task, fast presentation time and increased retention interval adversely affected recall for all subjects. Examination of the organizational output of the subjects suggests that different recall strategies are employed by the two age groups. In 'bunching' strategy, the hearing-impaired ten-year-olds are, again, equal to their normal hearing peers but the hearing-impaired six-year-olds are inferior to the normal hearing six-year-olds ($p < .001$). In agreement with previous research, mean picture memory span for the ten-year-old hearing-impaired and control subjects is four to five items per composite picture. There is a reduced mean picture memory span of two items for the six-year-old hearing-impaired subjects and three to four items for the six-year-old control subjects.

Date of Research: January 1983–Autumn 1985.

KEYWORDS: memory; hearing impairment; short-term memory; primary

Hester-Adrian Research Centre

See under Manchester University.

Ida Darwin Hospital, Cambridge

1/049 Ida Darwin Hospital
    Music Therapy Department
    Fulbourn
    Cambridge CB1 5EE
    Tel: 0223-880501 ext: 217

Oldfield, Amelia, Mrs; Adams, Malcolm
Supervisor: Bunt, L.

An investigation of the effects of music therapy on a group of profoundly mentally handicapped adults.

Background: The aim of this investigation is to find out how effective music therapy is in achieving a set of objectives when working with a group of severely mentally handicapped adults, and to compare the efficacy of music therapy to that of play activities.

Design: The study involves a group of 12 profoundly mentally handicapped people. Four subjects have been selected at random among them for intensive study and allocated randomly to two groups. The other subjects have been allocated at random to make up six in each of the two groups. One group has received weekly music therapy sessions for six months while the other has had a play session and this was then reversed for a further six months.

Sessions have been videotaped, concentrating on the four experimental subjects. The videotapes have now been analysed, using time sampling to record the occurrence of behaviour indicating the achievement of aims identified for each individual before the study.

In addition, observations have been made during the sessions to record how staff attention is distributed among the six members of each group.

Methods: For each subject three specific aims were selected and objective, observational measures were obtained for each of these. Data for each subject will be analysed individually. If music therapy is effective, then we would expect that for subjects in group A scores will increase during the first six months and then stay at the same level or decline, whereas for subjects in group B scores should stay the same for the first six months and then increase during the second period of the study. This set of individual analyses will be supplemented by a between-subject analysis.

Results: The results of this project will be submitted for publication. Since there is very little research into the effectiveness of music therapy the results will be of considerable interest, both clinically and for teaching purposes (for example, teaching music therapy students about research). Even if the results are negative because of the possible low power of this experiment, the study will still provide useful guidelines for further research.

Date of Research: January 1982–December 1984.

Published Material: OLDFIELD, A. and ADAMS, M. (1983). 'An investigation of the effects of music therapy on a group of profoundly mentally handicapped adults', *International Journal of Rehabilitation Research* (Heidelberg), **6**, 4, 511.

KEYWORDS: *music therapy; mental handicap; play; adult*

Inner London Education Authority

1/050   ILEA Research & Statistics Branch   Enquiries should be addressed to
           Addington Street Annexe   the Information Officer
           Addington Street
           County Hall
           London SE1 7UY

ILEA Language Census.

Background: The ILEA has reported on the languages spoken in ILEA schools in 1978, 1981 and 1983. However, until the 1983 survey, special schools were not included in the research.
Design: The survey covers all ILEA special schools, nursery, primary and secondary schools.
Methods: Teachers are asked to provide language information for all pupils on roll. Information is requested on (i) the home language other than English, Used by pupils in the school; (ii) the number of pupils using each language; (iii) for each language group, the number of pupils in each stage of English learning using a four-point scale.

Results: The latest survey, carried out in 1983, identified 147 different languages spoken in all the Authority's schools. 11.2 per cent of special school pupils spoke a language other than or in addition to English at home, compared with 15.2 per cent of nursery pupils, 18.9 per cent of primary pupils and 13.5 per cent of secondary pupils.

Date of Research: Biennial Survey.

Published Material: KYSEL, F. (1983). *Language Census*. London: Inner London Education Authority Research and Statistics (Report RS 916/83).

KEYWORDS: special school survey; English as a second language; language

1/051   ILEA Research & Statistics Branch   Enquiries should be addressed to
           Addington Street Annexe   the Information Officer.
           Addington Street
           County Hall
           London SE1 7UY

Special school examination results in the ILEA.

Background: The ILEA publishes an annual report on the examination results obtained by secondary school pupils. Since 1977, however, the results of pupils in special schools have not been involved. A report was therefore written to provide information on the public examination performance of pupils in special schools in 1982. This report formed the basis of an annual report which is now provided for schools sub-committee.
Design: The annual survey covers all special schools with secondary age pupils, except those for pupils with severe learning problems, hospital schools and schools for autistic pupils.
Methods: Headteachers are asked to complete a return for each pupil taking A- and O-level and CSE examinations specifying the candidate's name, sex, date of birth, the subjects and boards for which the pupil has been entered, the examination centre and final grades obtained.

Results: The latest report, covering examinations taken in 1982, indicates at CSE level a similar level of achievement to other ILEA secondary schools, although the performance in mathematics was less successful. At O-level the success rate was lower than that for ordinary schools and only three pupils entered for A-level.

Date of Research: Annual survey.

Published Material: COULTER, A. (1982). *Special Schools Examination Results 1981.* London: Inner London Education Authority Research and Statistics (Report RS 850/82). COULTER, A. (1983). *Special School Examination Results 1982.* London: Inner London Education Authority Research and Statistics (Report 912/83).

KEYWORDS: *special school survey; examination results; secondary*

1/052   ILEA Research & Statistics Branch   Enquiries should be addressed to
             Addington Street Annexe   the Information Officer
             Addington Street
             County Hall
             London SE1 7UY

A survey of pupils in ILEA special schools.

Background: The ILEA collects information about the background of pupils in primary and secondary schools in order to construct educational priority indices. Special schools have, up to now, not been included in this exercise. However, it was felt that if this information were also obtained for pupils in special education, useful comparisons could be made between all pupils in London schools. In addition, it was considered that this information should be seen in the context of children's specific disabilities as well as their educational needs.

Design: The survey covered all ILEA special schools and special units.

Methods: Headteachers were asked to complete a form for each child in an ILEA special school or unit. The information collected included the pupil's date of birth, sex, date of entry to school, ethnic and socio-economic background. In addition, a grid of disability/ special needs was completed under headings such as current cognitive functioning speech, language, physical mobility. Headteachers were also asked to assess the severity of the disability on a scale of mild, moderate and severe. Additional questions sought information on the condition from which the pupil suffered and on other educational problems, for example, the use of sign language.

Date of Research: Autumn 1983–Autumn 1984.

KEYWORDS: special school survey; education priority index; epidemiology

---

1/053   ILEA Research & Statistics Branch   Davies, Jean, Mrs
             County Hall   *Supervisor:* Mortimore, P., Dr
             London SE1 7PB   (Director ILEA Education
                                                       Research & Statistics Branch)

Support centre monitoring and evaluation programme: the reintegration of centre pupils into school.

Background: Research and statistics branch has been monitoring and evaluating the School Support Programme since its inception in September 1978. Basic descriptive information on support centres and their pupils is collected on a regular basis and more detailed studies are undertaken periodically to explore certain key issues in relation to the Programme. The present study explores the issue of the reintegration of pupils into school after a spell at the centre. The aims of the study are (1) to discover how pupils returning from off-site support centres are being reintegrated back into mainstream education and (2) to assess the extent to which this process is successful.

Design: Pupils (aged 11–14 years) leaving off-site support centres in ILEA, during spring and summer terms 1982, to return to their parent school.

Size: 158 pupils (the total population in this age-group returning to their own schools).

Methods: Interviews with pastoral care staff at receiving schools after pupils had been back in school for one whole term.

Register analysis to obtain information on the pupils' attendance before and after their stay in centres.

Date of Research: Spring 1982–Summer 1984.

KEYWORDS: *support centres; behaviour problem; reintegration; programme evaluation; secondary*

1/054	ILEA Research & Statistics Branch Room A313 County Hall Addington Street London SE1 Tel: 01-633-6350/2993	Jay, Elizabeth, Mrs; Kysel, Florrise, Ms

Survey of pupils in ILEA special schools and units.

Background: The aim of the survey is to obtain a description of pupils in special schools or units – with respect to age, sex, social and ethnic background, and disabilities. Of particular interest is the number of pupils suffering from multiple disabilities.

Design: The survey investigates the social and ethnic characteristics of special school population and the nature of the disabilities from which pupils suffer.

Size: All pupils in ILEA special schools and units (approx. 8000).

Methods: A form is completed for each pupil by the head of the special school/unit. This form asks for information on the pupil's age, sex, date of entry to school/unit, parental occupation, family size, family structure, eligibility for free school meals, ethnic group. Teachers are also asked to indicate the nature and degree of the pupil's disability/ies and the type of curriculum appropriate to the pupil.

Date of Research: July 1983–December 1984.

KEYWORDS: *incidence of special needs; special school survey*

Institute of Psychiatry

See under London University.

Jordanhill College of Education

1/055	Department of Special and Remedial Education Jordanhill College of Education Southbrae Drive Glasgow Tel: 041-959-1232	Browning, M., Mrs

Identifying and meeting the educational needs of profoundly mentally handicapped children.

Background: This was a collaborative venture between Jordanhill College, Strathclyde Region Education Department and the Scottish Council for Spastics. It aimed to identify and meet the educational needs of profoundly mentally handicapped children functioning at a mental age of less than one year. A multidisciplinary team (psychologist, teacher, instructress, physiotherapist, occupational therapist and speech therapist) investigated four main areas through case study work.
Design: The four areas were: Assessment; Teaching strategies and curriculum; The role of a multidisciplinary team; The establishment of a resource unit.
Size: Twelve profoundly mentally handicapped children.
Methods: Case study methods.

Results: Some success was recorded in the achievement of the aims established.

Date of Research: April 1980–March 1983.

Published Material: BROWNING, M.M., BAILEY, I.J. and CLARK, O. (1981). *Schools and Units for Profoundly Mentally Handicapped Children in the Strathclyde Region of Scotland.* Glasgow: Jordanhill College.
BROWNING, ANDERSON, BAILEY, LAW, MACLEOD and SUCKLING (1983). *Identifying and Meeting the Needs of Profoundly Mentally Handicapped Children.* Final report. Glasgow: Jordanhill College.

KEYWORDS: ESN(S); multidisciplinary; severe learning difficulties; assessment; curriculum development

1/056   Department of Special Educational   Browning, M., Mrs; Bailey, Irene
                 Needs   J., Mrs; Macleod, Catherine, Mrs
                 Jordanhill College of Education
                 Southbrae Drive
                 Glasgow G13 1PP
                 Tel: 041-959-1232

Identifying and meeting the needs of profoundly mentally handicapped children.

Background: This project was concerned with assessment and curriculum development for children with profound mental and multiple impairments.
Design: The assessment and development was done by a multi-disciplinary team of educational psychologists, teachers, instructors, physiotherapist, speech therapist and occupational therapist.
Size: Nine children living at home and attending nine schools.
Methods: Through action research the team developed an approach to assessment and the development and implementation of a concept of curriculum. The curriculum was based on meeting the assessed needs of the children through a planned series of learning experiences resulting from informed judgments about content, teaching/learning strategies, learning environments and resources.

Results: Applications of the team's approach did produce situations in which objectives for children were reached.

Date of Research: 1979–March 1983.

Published Material: BROWNING, M.M. *et al.* (1983). *Identifying and Meeting the Needs of Profoundly Mentally Handicapped Children.* Glasgow: Jordanhill College.
BAILEY, I.J. (1983). *Structuring a Curriculum for Profoundly Mentally Handicapped Children.* Glasgow: Jordanhill College.

ANDERSON, C.A. (1983). *Feeding: a Guide to Assessment and Intervention with Handicapped Children*. Glasgow: Jordanhill College.
LAW, I.H. and SUCKLING, M.H. (1983). *Handling When Children are Profoundly Handicapped*. Glasgow: Jordanhill College.

KEYWORDS: profound mental handicap; severe learning difficulties; assessment; curriculum development; multiple handicap

Keele University

1/057	Department of Psychology University of Keele Keele Staffs ST5 5BG Tel: 0782-621111	Combes, Gill, Ms *Supervisor:* Hegarty, J., Dr

The drinking patterns and beliefs of ESN(M) schoolchildren and their implications for health education.

Background: To assess the special needs of slow learners for health education about alcohol, arising from their educational abilities, drinking patterns and social backgrounds.
Size: 144 slow learners, in main study (from ESN(M) schools) aged 9–16.
Methods: One-to-one interviews with slow learners. A series of game-like tasks was used to assess children's knowledge of, opinions about, and experiences of drinking alcohol. Questionnaires for teachers to assess children's academic and social backgrounds and to detail school health education practices. Follow-up of small group of children, 18 months after leaving school.

Results: Special needs for alcohol education were identified, primarily in the design and approach of teaching materials. A number of risk factors were identified in children's social backgrounds which implied future risks of heavy or problem drinking.

Date of Research: October 1981–June 1984.

KEYWORDS: alcohol; health education; ESN(M)

1/058	Department of Psychology University of Keele Keele Staffs ST5 5BG Tel: 0782-621111	McDonald, John *Supervisor:* Hegarty, J., Dr

The nature, assessment and development of 'numeracy' in low ability children.

Background: To produce a refined scale of assessment (individually administered) of numeracy suitable for backward children, and to deploy this in monitoring the efficacy of computer presented number development programmes.
Design: Survey and experiment.
Size: 200 children (aprox.) in obtaining 'age norms' from the assessment scale and 30 ESN(M) children (approx.) in examining the results of computer assisted learning.

Date of Research: January 1982–December 1985 (for PhD at Keele University).

KEYWORDS: numeracy; ESN(M); assessment; computer assisted learning

King Alfred's College, Winchester

1/059   Special Education and Habilitation   Hughes, G.B.; Hughes, Geoffrey
           Unit   *Supervisor:* Jackson, R.N., Dr
           King Alfred's College
           Winchester
           Tel: 0962-62281

A rural crafts centre for Hampshire for the next decade.

Background: MENCAP currently supports the Blendworth Country Centre which is based on the pioneering work of Lufton Manor Rural Training Centre and provides for post school education of mentally handicapped youngsters.

Recent changes in attitudes, alternative provision, and changing patterns of employment require that current practices be re-examined in the light of these factors.

Design: Current provision at Blendworth is being examined in the light of practice at similar establishments which are supported by LEAs and Social Services (e.g. ATCs).

Size: Eight Rural Training Units (or similar establishments). Four Adult Training Centres. A 'snowball' sample of information.

Methods: Informal interviews are being conducted with suitable informants and this is being combined with a series of site visits.

Date of Research: September 1984–February 1985.

KEYWORDS: mental handicap; rural studies; crafts; post-school; horticulture; adult training centre

Lancashire Polytechnic

1/060   School of Combined Studies   Hurst, Alan
           Lancashire Polytechnic   *Supervisor:* Tomlinson, Sally,
           Corporation Street   Prof.
           Preston PR1 2TQ
           Tel: 0772-22141 ext. 2475

Higher education and physical Handicap: an interactionist approach.

Background: One sector of the population whose needs in further and higher education are met inadequately are the physically impaired. Contemporary social trends and the cutbacks in education could make the situation worse. With the rise in unemployment plus the increase in the size of the group applying for a restricted number of places in higher education, there is a need for a new investigation – hence the present project. The aim is to discover how young people with physical impairments fare in the increasingly difficult struggle to secure a place at univeristy, polytechnic, college of higher education – how the admissions procedures work, which institutions and which courses are chosen and why, and so on.

Design: The project envisaged is a long-term, longitudinal study which falls into two major parts. The first of these will begin by identifying a suitable sample. The second part will follow a small number of the successful applicants through their higher education courses.

Size: Given the possible range of physical impairments, the focus will be on those whose problems relate to mobility and access. (Students with sensory handicaps are outside the scope of the present study.) The main sample will consist of between ten and 15 individuals.

Methods: Throughout, the emphasis of the research method is on meeting and talking with people to generate information for interpretation and discussion. The theoretical perspective underpinning the project and to be employed in the analysis of the data produced is interactionist. Symbolic interaction tries to explain how man comes to 'know' the world; this occurs in contexts involving other people. The emphasis is upon the dynamic aspects of interpersonal relations and the ways in which individuals can change and modify their behaviour in relation to the perceptions of each other. Within this theoretical framework there are a number of concepts: self; identity; role; status; norms; expectations; significant others; etc.

Date of Research: September 1983 – December 1988.

Published Material: HURST, H.A. (1984a). 'Legislation in special education', *Special Education, Forward Trends*, **11**, 1.
HURST, H.A. (1984b). 'Adolescence and physical impairment: an interactionist approach'. In: Barton, L. and Tomlinson, S. (Eds) *Special Education and Social Interests.* London: Croom Helm.

KEYWORDS: physical handicap; higher education; school leaver

Lancaster University

1/061   Centre for Educational Research &   Badger, Bill
            Development   *Supervisors:* O'Hare, Eric;
            Department of Educational Research   Bennett, Neville, Prof.
            University of Lancaster
            Lancaster LA1 4YL
            Tel: 0524-65201 ext. 4865

In-school approaches to the problem of disruptive behaviour.

Background: Cumbria offered a year's teacher-fellowship at Lancaster to follow up earlier work on behavioural problems in the county's schools. Having been offered the fellowship, I have worked from a 'school-differences' standpoint, referring to Rutter, Lawrence, Reynolds *et al.*, and have looked at *school* effects on levels of disruption.
Design: Narrowed down to a case-study approach of one school after a general survey of current provision for, and approaches to, disruptive behaviour.
Size: One 1300 pupil comprehensive school in West Cumbria.
Methods: Non-observational monitoring of disruptive events; analysis of school documents, extensive staff and pupil interviews; 14 approaches in total; a two-week pilot study followed by a four-week full study – two months in-school work.

Results: A 95-page report to the school indicating that a number of school 'processes' appear to have a direct bearing on levels of disruption. Much depends on school reaction as to 'results'.

Date of Research: September 1983 – Report to county June 1984.

KEYWORDS: school processes; behaviour problem; secondary

1/062   Centre for Educational Research &   Hadfield, S., Mrs
             Development   *Supervisors:* Bennett, Neville,
             Department of Educational Research   Prof.; O'Hare, Eric
             University of Lancaster
             Lancaster LA1 4YL
             Tel: 0524-65201 ext. 4865

Integration of pupils with speical needs into ordinary schools (moderate learning difficulties).

Background: For a number of years, special schools have been returning pupils to mainstream education. Recently, the number of such transfers appears to be increasing. In many cases the transfer appears to have been successful. However, there may have been problems which were overcome when only a small number of pupils were concerned, but which may prove to be barriers to the success of integration if larger numbers of pupils were to be transferred. The purpose of this research is to study the transfer of pupils from special to ordinary schools in order to identify factors which contribute to successful integration and problems involved in transfer, particularly in relation to (a) the way in which pupils cope with the curriculum; (b) the pupil's socialization; (c) the effect on the ordinary school.

Design: It is proposed to make in-depth case studies of pupils who will be transferring to ordinary schools during the academic year 1983–4 and to follow them through the transfer process.

Methods: Discussions with teachers concerned in both ordinary and special schools. Discussions with other persons concerned in the process of integration, e.g. headteachers, liaison teachers, educational psychologists, support teachers. Observations of pupils in both special and ordinary schools, immediately prior to and following transfer. Observations at regular intervals after transfer. One term after transfer, discussions with head, class teacher, pupils and parents.

Date of Research: April 1983–April 1985.

KEYWORDS: *integration; moderate learning difficulties; transfer of pupils*

1/063   Department of Educational Research   Bennett, Neville, Prof.
             University of Lancaster
             Lancaster LA1 4YL
             Tel: 0524-65201

The integration of ESN(M) children into normal schools.

Background: (1) To ascertain policy and practice on integration in 17 North Western LEAs. (2) To ascertain issues in the transfer process pertinent to: (a) The development of theory; (b) The development of in-service and pre-service courses for teachers.

Design: (1) Interviews with advisors/educational psychologists in 17 LEAs. (2) Follow up of samples of ESN(M) children from special through to normal schools.

Size: (1) 17 LEAs. (2) Depends on outcomes of (1), i.e. how many children are being integrated.

Methods: (1) Interviews. (2) Observation of social and task related behaviours; description of curriculum experiences; peer interaction; interviews with teachers and parents.

Date of Research: January 1984–December 1985.

KEYWORDS: *integration; ESN(M); curriculum continuity; teacher training; in-service education*

1/064   Department of Educational Research   Tomlinson, Sally, Prof.
           University of Lancaster
           Lancaster LA1 4YL
           Tel: 0524-65201

Ethnic minorities and special education.

Background: Examination of the issues and problems that arise when children from other racial and cultural backgrounds are offered a special education in Britain.
Design: Small-scale, case studies to illustrate issues.
Methods: Interviews, observations, content analysis of files.

Date of Research: 1984 – ongoing.

KEYWORDS: ethnic minorities; educational provision.

Leeds Polytechnic

1/065   School of Education   Freeman, Alan
           Leeds Polytechnic   *Supervisors:* Robson, C., Dr;
           Becket Park   Newbold, D., Dr
           Leeds LS6 3QS
           Tel: 0532-759061

A study of curriculum content in schools for children with severe learning difficulties.

Background: To develop an understanding of curriculum content through a descriptive study attempting to answer the following research questions:
(1) Which areas of curriculum content are most commonly used in ESN(S) schools?
(2) How do teachers in ESN(S) schools perceive the relative importance of these areas of curriculum content?
Design: Twelve schools for children with severe learning difficulties made up of four Hospital Schools, four purpose built schools and four schools originally built as training centres.
Size: Three teachers within each school, 36 teachers, currently teaching children in the under 9 years, 9 to 13 years or 13 years plus age-range.
Methods: Mail questionnaire; analysis of available curricula; personal interview; paired comparison.

Results: The following 13 areas of curriculum content were identified as being commonly used in ESN(S) schools: Socializing Inside; Language; Play; Music; P.E. & Movement; Socializing Outside; Art & Craft; Storytelling & Drama; Number; Domestic Skills; Nature; Reading and Writing. The danger of treating these curriculum areas on the basis of a simple ranking were emphasized when changes in importance with the age of child were taken into account. Statistically significant increases of importance with the age of child were noted for Domestic Skills, Reading and Writing, whilst Play, Music and Storytelling & Drama showed a significant decrease.

Date of Research: 1978 – 1983.

KEYWORDS: curriculum content; severe learning difficulties; ESN(S); special school survey

Leeds University

1/066   School of Education   Barnes, D.R.
           University of Leeds
           Leeds LS2 9JT
           Tel: 0532-31751

A study of 'personal and social' elements in the curricula of special schools.

Background: This is an informal study being carried out with the help of teachers who are seconded to courses in this university. The aim is to throw light on how teachers in special schools perceive their pupils and their own responsibilities for their social and personal development.

Design: We have begun with interviews and osbervation in a limited number of schools, but the range may expand as the study develops.

Date of Research: February 1984 – open-ended.

KEYWORDS: personal development; social education; special school curriculum

1/067   School of Education   Moore, Alan
           University of Leeds   *Supervisors:* Sharp, P., Dr;
           Leeds LS2 9JT   Sugden, D., Dr
           Tel: 0532-31751

The changing role and curriculum of the ESN(S) school 1970 – 1983.

Background: In the light of recent philosophical and legislative changes, the nature of the ESN(S) school has changed radically since 1970. The role and the curriculum of the ESN(S) school reflect these interconnected changes.

Design: The investigation looked at philosophical changes as reflected in Journals and Educational Reports.

Methods: Study of Educational Journals; study of school curriculum documents; study of reports on special education; chronological reporting method used.

Date of Research: January 1983 – December 1983.

KEYWORDS: special school role; curriculum; ESN(S); philosophy; resource centre; severe learning difficulties.

1/068   School of Education   Sugden, D.A., Dr
           University of Leeds
           Leeds LS2 9JT
           Tel: 0532-31751

The transfer of cognitive strategies in children with moderate learning difficulties.

Background: There is good evidence to suggest children with moderate learning difficulties do not easily transfer material learned in one area for use in another. This investigation examines methods of facilitating this process.

Size: Children with moderate learning difficulties aged 9 – 12.

Methods: Children will be taught memory strategies such as rehearsal, semantic elaboration, organization, logical research. At first maintenance (retention) will be the aim. Then the children will be taught to examine tasks to determine their demand and apply the appropriate strategy. Finally, generalization will be examined. It is hoped to generate some curriculum based materials from this.

The investigation will take the form of instructional approach working with individuals rather than group analysis.

Date of Research: Pilot January 1984, actual September 1984–Ongoing.

KEYWORDS: moderate learning difficulties; primary; curriculum development; cognitive strategies.

1/069	School of Education University of Leeds Leeds LS2 9JT Tel: 0532-31751	Sugden, D.A., Dr

A comparison of two assessment procedures for children with movement problems.

Design: Two recent assessment methods (Henderson revision of Stott Test of Motor Impairment, and Laszlo and Bairstow Kinaesthetic Assessment) are being compared on a group of children with learning difficulties. Incidence of problems will be established together with individual profiles on both tests.

Size: 7/8 year olds–35
11/12 year olds–35
Methods: As per manuals.

Date of Research: February 1984–Ongoing.

KEYWORDS: assessment; motor problems; learning difficulties

Leicester University

1/070	School of Education University of Leicester 21 University Rd. Leicester LE1 7RF Tel: 0533-551122	Hunter, Morag, Miss; Merry, Roger, Dr

Learning Difficulties Project (Coalville area).

Background: Teachers approached University for help in assessing special needs in their area. Discussion led to a headteacher being seconded for a year, then a series of one-term fellowships, for collaborative work to identify good practice.

Design: Initially compared local sample to national survey of Bernbaum and Croll. Now looking at ideas for helping these children, compiled in a compendium of materials.

Size: 336 children initially tested, then structured interviews with 20 teachers and about 66 of the children (all 2nd or 4th year juniors).

Methods: As above, i.e. used standardized tests and structured interviews in an 'Action Research' design, working jointly with teachers, through meetings and visits. Seconded teachers now work in all 8 schools, producing materials and newsletters.

Results: Interim trends: greater contact between schools; better understanding of collaborative research; 13 newsletters so far; more use of LEA resources and expertise.

Date of Research: Sept. 81 – Research ongoing. Aim is a compendium of practical materials rather than a report.

Published Material: HUNTER, C.M. (1984). 'Meeting Teachers' Special Needs Through Collaborative Research'. Paper published in 1984 in the report on 1983 UKRA conference. DENNIS, D. (Ed) *Reading: meeting children's special needs.* London: Heinemann ed. books.

KEYWORDS: teacher-based research; curriculum development; learning difficulties; primary

1/071	School of Education	McNicol, Heather, Ms
	University of Leicester	*Supervisor:* Merry, R., Dr
	21 University Rd.	
	Leicester LE1 7RF	
	Tel: 0533-551122	

Factors influencing later adjustment: a comparison of leavers from residential special schools for maladjusted boys.

Background: To draw attention to those factors in the way special schools for maladjusted children operate which have a positive effect on the children's later adjustment. To emphasize that the only way a special school for the maladjusted can be assessed is by looking at how 'adjusted' the children are after leaving the school.
Design: A detailed study of approximately 30 boys – retrospective and prospective. Surveys of other schools to provide a comparison for the above.
Size: Thirty boys studied in detail. Other children's progress reported in questionnaires by their schools.
Methods: Questionnaires; structured and unstructured interviews; surveys.

Date of Research: October 1983 – 1987 – 8 (Estimated).

KEYWORDS: maladjustment; disturbed pupil; residential special school; school leaver.

1/072	School of Education	Smith, Sandra L., Miss
	University of Leicester	*Supervisors:* Merry, Roger, Dr;
	21 University Road	Hunter, Morag
	Leicester LE1 7RF	
	Tel: 0533-551122	

A pilot scheme to establish the feasibility of creating a bank of items, related to life skills, for the assessment of 15 – 16 + pupils' reading ability.

Background: The research is investigating the possibility of making statements about the reading abilities of less able 15 – 16 + pupils other than the usual form of reading age. The majority of reading attainment tests sample only a few of the major dimensions of reading, and can be said to be poor indicators of pupils' ability to use reading skills in a variety of situations, especially those which can be termed 'real life'.
Design: The development of items consisting of criterion-referenced tasks requiring pupil response to materials and situations which an ordinary member of the community has to cope with in everyday life. Pupil response will be assessed on a 'can do' basis. Pupils will also be expected to provide information about their reading preferences in terms of materials and activities utilized for the items. This might establish if such preference can influence interaction with the text and comprehension of the task.

Size: 66–69 15 + pupils receiving attention in SEN Departments in Warwickshire Secondary Schools and Mild Learning Difficulties Schools.

Methods: Pre-testing of items, from two or three of the General Task Objective areas established, with pupils in a general classroom situation.

Date of Research: September 1983–1985.

KEYWORDS: reading; item bank; assessment; criterion-referencing; secondary; life skills

London University

1/073   Birkbeck College   Casey, Wendy Dr (Harperbury
        University of London   Hospital, Radlett, Herts.);
        Malet Street   Watkins, Brian J. (Tetherdown
        London WC1E 7HX   Child Guidance Centre, London
        Tel: 01-580-6622   N10)
                                             Supervisors: Jones, David, Dr
                                             (Birkbeck College); Casey,
                                             Wendy, Dr; Watkins, Brian J.

Haringey Down's Syndrome Project.

Background: As a Local Education Authority, Haringey has been giving active consideration to integrating Down's Syndrome children in mainstream schools. This study is designed as an exploratory investigation as to how such integration could be best achieved.

Design: It was proposed to monitor the progress of Down's children in different educational settings over a two-year period, the settings being: (a) mainstream schools; (b) ESN(M) schools; (c) ESN(S) schools.

Size: (a) Mainstream school – 20 children, age 4–8, mixed; (b) ESN(M) school – 20 children, age 4–8, mixed; (c) ESN(S) school – 20 children, age 4–8, mixed.

Methods: Assessment at six-monthly intervals by means of standardized tests. Interviews with Teachers, Head Teachers and parents, no recording of test results being made until end of project.

Date of Research: January 1983–January 1986.

KEYWORDS: integration; ESN(M); ESN(S); Down's syndrome

1/074   Centre for Science & Mathematics   Denvir, Brenda, Mrs
        Education   *Supervisor:* Brown, Margaret, Dr
        Chelsea College
        Bridges Place
        London SW6 4HR
        Tel: 01-736-3401

The development of number concepts in low attainers in mathematics aged 7–9 years.

Background: This research reports a series of studies with low attainers in mathematics in the primary school.
The aims of the research were to develop a framework for describing low attainers'

acquistion of number concepts, to use the framework to develop a diagnostic assessment instrument, to use the results of administering the diagnostic assessment instrument to low attainers alongside the descriptive framework as a basis for designing remedial teaching programmes, and to gain insight into the teaching and learning of number concepts.
Design: In developing the descriptive framework a study was made of which skills are prerequisites for other skills and hence the extent to which the descriptive framework is hierarchical.
Methods: Interviewing techniques were used to assess which skills the pupils had acquired. These techniques and the hierarchical framework were then used to develop a Diagnostic Assessment Interview. Results of this Interview were analysed and interpreted to show how the children's performance could be used to assign the skills which were assessed to one of six levels of difficulty and the pupils who were interviewed to one of six levels of performance. Two teaching studies were carried out, using the descriptive framework as a basis.

Date of Research: October 1981–September 1984.

Published Material: DENVIR, B. (1982). 'Simple Questions and Complicated Answers', *Struggle: Mathematics for Low Attainers*, **9,** ILEA.
DENVIR, B., STOLZ, C. and BROWN, M. (1981). *Low Attainers in Mathematics 5–16: Policies and Practices in Schools.* London: Methuen.

KEYWORDS: number concepts; low attainer; diagnostic assessment; remedial teaching; primary.

1/075   Faculty of Education   Machin, Janet, Ms
               Kings College London   *Supervisor:* Aspin, David, Prof.
               Strand
               London WC2R 2LS
               Tel: 01-836-5454

Identification and assessment of the philosophical basis of curriculum development and implementation for special needs education.

Background: Aim in LEA to establish the nature of education and philosophy in special education.
Design: Just commenced. Investigation design being established.
Methods: Review of current UK publications/conference materials – structured interviews with interested parties. Initial survey of London schools.

Date of Research: March 1984–March 1987.

KEYWORDS: philosophy; curriculum development.

1/076   Department of Developmental   Sonksen, Patricia, Dr
               Paediatrics
               London University Institute of
               Child Health
               30 Guildford Street
               London WC1N IEH
               Tel: 01-242-9789

The provision of optimal visual experience for development in babies and pre-school children with severe visual disabilities.

Background: The research aims to develop a paediatric scheme of visual assessment which dovetails developmental and functional aspects with the more standard optical measures used by opthalmologists, orthoptists and opthalmic opticians, so that the findings can be used: (i) to prescribe practical guidance for the promotion of further visual development; (ii) together with the developmental profile determined by comprehensive developmental assessment, to prescribe optimal visual conditions and experiences for general development; and (iii) to prescribe the most appropriate optical and other low vision aids for the enhancement of vision in relation to current developmental functioning.

Design: A variety of tests and visual management programmes are evaluated and the use of low vision aids for this age group investigated.

Date of Research: May 1983–May 1988.

Published Material: SONKSEN, P.M. (1982). *The Assessment of 'Vision for Development' in Severely Handicapped Babies.*

KEYWORDS: *visual impairment; assessment; optical aids; development*

<table>
<tr><td>1/077</td><td>Department of Child Development and Educational Psychology University of London Institute of Education Bedford Way London WC1H 0AL Tel: 01-636-1500 ext. 792</td><td>Bowman, Irene, Mrs Supervisors: Bowman, Irene; Wedell, Klaus, Prof., Allinson, Olive</td></tr>
</table>

A 15-country questionnaire survey of pre- and in-service training needs for teachers serving in ordinary schools where there are children with special needs.

Background: This research comprises stages one and two of a five-stage UNESCO project, designed to generate approaches to training teachers in the education of children with special needs. The emphasis is upon teacher competencies for integration.

Methods: Production of two questionnaires, to be translated and sent to 15 countries (three in each of UNESCO's five regions). One questionnaire is for a named person in each country, and seeks information on national policy, legislation and practice. The other is for a sample of 100 teachers (primary, secondary, etc.) in each country, and seeks information on their training, experience of pupils with special needs, their views on integration, their perceived areas of competence and weakness, their preference for pedagogy, and their perceived needs for training. Countries are also asked to submit a report on one example of good practice which might be of use to other countries.

Results: Report due in July 1984

Date of Research: June 1983–July 1984.

KEYWORDS: *teacher training; in-service education; integration; international comparison*

<table>
<tr><td>1/078</td><td>Department of Child Development & Educational Psychology University of London Institute of Education 24–27 Woburn Square London WC1H 0AA Tel: 01-636-1500</td><td>Evans, Peter, Dr Supervisors: Wedell, K., Prof.; Skilbeck, M., Prof. (Dept. of Curriculum Studies)</td></tr>
</table>

Research and development on the curriculum for pupils with moderate learning difficulties.

Background: The project will focus on curriculum development in terms of the formulation of objectives and on the monitoring of the progress of pupils with moderate learning difficulties in special and ordinary schools, whether in units or other forms of provision. The aim of the project will be to develop procedures by which schools can formulate appropriate aspects of their curricular aims and content in terms of objectives, and can monitor these pupils' progress.

Design: The research will investigate how such innovation can be implemented in schools, and within the limits of duration and scale of the project will evaluate the outcome for pupils and schools. Curriculum development guidelines and in-service training materials will also be derived from the project.

Date of Research: January 1985–June 1988.

KEYWORDS: moderate learning difficulties; curriculum development

1/079   Department of Child Development &   Evans, P. Dr; Ware, J.E., Ms
             Educational Psychology
             University of London Institute of
             Education
             26 Woburn Square
             London WC1H 0AA
             Tel: 01-636-1500

Education of the profoundly handicapped.

Methods: The project is divided into two parts. In the first a limited survey will be carried out of special care units (SCU) catering for profoundly mentally handicapped children in the S.E. of England. Data from this survey will be used to select schools for study in the second part. The second part involves the collection of detailed classroom obeservation data in four main areas: teacher child interactions; classroom management; child engagement; and the duration of individual programme implementation. Apart from the analysis of these variables in their own right the intention is to relate indicators of these variables to estimates of behaviour change in the children. The study involves two assessments of the development of the children with a 12 month interval between each and three assessments of the classroom-based measures at six monthly intervals in order to assess stability. This data will be analysed using generalized linear modelling procedures.

Date of Research: January 1984–December 1986.

KEYWORDS: special care unit; cognitive development; severe learning difficulties; classroom management

1/080   Department of Child Development &   Francis, Hazel, Prof.
             Educational Psychology
             University of London Institute of
             Education
             24–27 Woburn Square
             London WC1H 0AA
             Tel: 01-636-1500

Learning to read – problems and strategies.

Background: To explore metacognitive and cognitive problems and strategies of learning to read in normal and slow learners.

Design: Case study over three years, supplemented with experimental investigation.
Size: Starting at five years of age. Ten children, disadvantaged area, for case studies; 28 children, two schools, contrasting areas, for experimental study.
Methods: Observational and experimental.

Date of Research: 1976–1984.

Published Material: 1977 – 'Children's Strategies in Learning to Read', *British Journal of Educational Psychology*, 47, 117–125.
1982 – *Learning to Read – Literate Behaviour and Orthographic Knowledge*. London: Allen & Unwin.
1984 – 'Children's Knowledge of Orthography in Learning to Read', *British Journal of Educational Psychology*, 54, 8–23.

KEYWORDS: *beginning reading; orthography; reading.*

1/081   Department of Child Development &   Norwich, B., Dr
                Educational Psychology
                University of London Institute of
                Education
                25 Woburn Square
                London WC1H 0AA
                Tel: 01-636-1500

The aims of primary education for all children; a study of teacher and teacher trainee opinions.

Background: The aim of the study was to investigate the question whether teachers judged educational aims and goals to be the same for all children. Of particular interest was the question whether educational goals would be judged to be the same for children in ordinary schools and special schools for children with moderate learning difficulties (ESN(M)).
Design: Attitude questionnaire of relative evaluation of a set of educational aims/goals relevant to primary curriculum. Comparison of two groups under three different instruction conditions. Random allocation to conditions – 1. Ordinary School; 2. ESN(M) school; 3. MLD school – as contexts for evaluating aims/goals.
Size: 35 PGCE primary trainees (all students in one year) plus 35 special needs diploma students (random selection of half students in one year).

Results: 1) Similar rank order of educational goals for overall sample and two sub-groups found compared to previous study.
2) Some differences in relative evaluation of goals for Diploma students: e.g. personal adjustment goal perceived as less important for MLD special school than ordinary school; all other goals of similar evaluation levels.
3) For PGCE trainees aesthetic and basic educational skills were evaluated as less important in special school context. Analysis incomplete.

Date of Research: November 1983–October 1984.

KEYWORDS: *moderate learning difficulties; primary curriculum; ESN(M); teacher training; aims of education*

1/082   Department of Child Development &   Pauli, Margaret E., Ms
            Educational Psychology   *Supervisor:* Hindley, C.B., Prof.
            University of London Institute of
            Education
            24 – 27 Woburn Square
            London WC1H 0AA
            Tel: 01-636-1500

Personality and self-concept in physically handicapped children in day and residential schools.

Background: The research undertaking arose out of a pilot study which indicated some interesting differences in self-concept in physically handicapped children in day & residential school settings, using a repertory grid method of measurement. It was decided to examine self-concept and wider aspects of personality in similar groups under more controlled conditions.

Design: The study used groups of physically handicapped and normal children, drawn from a number of different schools in different parts of Southern England. The groups were used for comparative purposes regarding presence or absence of handicap, and day or residential schooling. All the disabled children were in segregated special schools.

Size: Four groups of 40 + children, aged ten to 14 years, matched overall for sex, age, and intellectual ability (vocabulary). The non-handicapped children formed the control groups.

Methods: A repertory grid technique was used to measure constructs consisting of ideal and actual self, together with commonly used social/emotional constructs such as friends, happy, discontented, etc. The strength of the relationship between these constructs forms the basis of the technique. Further personality measures included the Junior Eysenck Personality Questionnaire, the Attitude toward Disabled Persons Scale, and a measure of independence or self-help for the disabled groups. Statistical analysis included Slater's INGRID and COIN programmes, correlational analysis, and multivariate analysis.

Results: Striking differences were found between the groups in the repertory grid analysis, with the residential physically handicapped group obtaining lower construct correlations than all the other groups. Examination of the results indicated the suggestion that these children were consistent in their construct choices (as were the other groups), but were less discriminating in terms of the clarity of their construct relationships. There was little evidence of a link between the repertory grid results and the other personality measures, although these also revealed some group differences.

Date of Research: January 1979 – December 1984.

KEYWORDS: *self concept; repertory grid; physical handicap; personality; residential school; secondary*

1/083   Department of Child Development &   Sharpe, Pamela J. (College of St
            Educational Psychology   Mark & St John, Plymouth)
            University of London Institute of   *Supervisors:* Henderson, Sheila,
            Education   Dr; Versey, John, Dr
            24 – 27 Woburn Square
            London WC1H 0AA
            Tel: 01-636-1500

A study of the abilities of multiply disabled children.

Background: To assess the usefulness of an infant psychological development scale (IPDS) to multiply disabled children.

To produce profiles of the children's early cognitive behaviour in terms of sensori-motor schemes. Recent research has demonstrated that an IPDS devised by Uzgiris and Hunt produces valid results with profoundly mentally handicapped children. The scales are designed to reveal structural and hierarchical properties of emerging cognitive abilities. Since children with physical handicaps (severe) are labelled unassessable from psychometric tests it is envisaged that modifications of eliciting situations may reveal cognitive functioning which can be identified using qualitative data.

Design: Working for some time with multiply PH children revealed that inadequate testing techniques gave nil indications of abilities which teachers could describe. Thus detailed observations are made during provision of eliciting situations. These are recorded using video and other observers and transcribed onto the IPDS scales. Profiles reveal highest behaviour on each scale.

Size: 44 multiply (PH) disabled children and 23 able-bodied. The disabled children range between 12 months and 11 years and are selected in response to teachers' descriptions as unassessable on psychologists' reports. Able-bodied children aged five weeks to two years.

Methods: A one-to-one observation with experimenter following the manual of tasks modified from IPDS.

The groups of tasks permit realistic play situations with a range of objects and games which can be adapted to the special requirements of each child. The final manual has been devised as a result of observing one group of children over two years then observing responses of four other groups in other parts of the country and one group of able-bodied children.

Results: Further details available by January 1985. These are currently being analysed and the research written up but it appears that meaningful profiles of abilities are possible; that these are supported by teachers' observations; that interobserver agreement is high; thus it is possible to identify abilities and to devise realistic individualized intervention programmes.

Date of Research: 1980–January 1985.

Published Material: SHARPE, P.J. (1983) The Contribution of Individually Structured Play Experiences to the Cognitive Development of a Group of Multiply Physically Handicapped Infants. Paper presented to International Federation of Adapted Physical Activity, West London Institute of Higher Education, September, 1983.

KEYWORDS: multiple handicap; physical handicap; cognition; assessment; individualized instruction; development scale

1/084   Department of Curriculum Studies   Griffiths, John
           University of London Institute of   *Supervisors:* Walsh, P.D.; Simons,
           Education   H., Miss
           20 Bedford Way
           London WC1H 0AL
           Tel: 01-636-1500

Knowledge, structure and curricula for children with mild, moderate and severe learning difficulties.

Background: (i) To describe life in special classrooms; (ii) To describe *what* teachers in special classrooms teach, i.e. to focus on the content of the curriculum; (iii) To illuminate the beliefs, assumptions and intentions behind teachers' practice and particular selection of knowledge; (iv) To generate grounded theory about the nature, selection and organization of knowledge in special classrooms.

Design: Three qualitative case studies of at least half a term duration in each classroom.
Size: Three classrooms: (i) Eight children with profound & multiple handicaps in a classroom in a sub-normality hospital – + their teacher. (ii) Nine children and their teacher in a classroom in an ESN(S) school. (iii) Fifteen children and their teacher in an ESN(M) school.
Methods: Case study – using participant observation, interviews, questionnaires and discussion. Fieldwork completed September 1982 – July 1983.

Date of Research: October 1978 – Unable to estimate (has to be completed in ten years – six used up).

Published Material: GRIFFITHS, J. (1980). 'Special Education: in search of a concept', *Apex* (Journal of Brit. Inst. of Mental Handicap), **8,** 1, June 80.
GRIFFITHS, J. (1981). 'Gone Sailing – Curriculum at Sea', *Apex* (Journal of Brit. Inst. of Mental Handicap), **9,** 2, September 1981.
GRIFFITHS, J. (1983). 'Life in a Special Classroom'. *Mental Handicap* (formerly *Apex*), **11,** 1, March 1983.
GRIFFITHS, J. (1984a). 'Eggy Bread and Paddy's Bacon – instances of the traffic in knowledge in a classroom for children with severe language difficulties', *Journal of Curriculum Studies*, **16,** 1, Jan 84.
GRIFFITHS, J. (1984b). 'Special Education and a Curriculum Grow Bag', *Links*, Feb 1984.

KEYWORDS: curriculum development; moderate learning difficulties; severe learning difficulties; organization of knowledge; subnormality hospital

1/085   Department of Economic,   Goacher, Brian; Evans, Jennifer,
             Administrative and Policy Studies in   Ms
             Education   *Supervisors:* Welton, J., Dr
             University of London Institute of   (Director); Wedell, K., Prof.
             Education   (Director)
             59 Gordon Square
             London WC1H 0AL
             Tel: 01-636-1500

The 1981 Education Act: policy and provision for special needs project.

Background: The 1981 Education Act came into force in April 1983. From this date, the procedures for the identification and assessment of children with special needs and the provision of suitable education for these children up to the age of 19 have undergone a radical change.
The project will explore the response of LEAs to the demands and opportunities provided by the new legislation. It will: (1) see how the Act is affecting the work of administrators, educationalists and professional workers; (2) assess the effectiveness of the Act for giving children access to provision appropriate to their special needs; (3) identify 'good practice' in respect of both assessment and provision for special needs; (4) disseminate information about the workings of the Act to help all those who are concerned with it.
Design: The research will be carried out in three stages:
Stage 1 will consist of individual and group discussions with teachers, professionals in the Health Service, psychologists, doctors, social workers, administrators, voluntary groups, parents and children.
Stage 2 will involve more detailed discussion, observation and the collection of other evidence in a number of local authorities.
Stage 3 will include a national survey, carried out to determine the relevance of the

findings from the detailed studies and to assess the range of policies and practices in England and Wales.

Methods: Focussed interview, observation, questionnaire.

Results: The findings of the project will offer practical assistance to local authorities and schools in their task of ensuring that children with special educational needs are given suitable educational provision.

Date of Research: September 1983–September 1986

Published Material: GOACHER, B. (1984). 'Policy and provision for special needs project', *British Psychological Society Division of Education and Child Psychology Newsletter*, 14 May.

KEYWORDS: policy; Education Act 1981; educational provision; assessment

| 1/086 | University of London Institute of Education
18 Woburn Square
London WC1H 0NS
Tel: 01-636-1500 ext. 298 | Gipps, Caroline, Dr; Gross, Harriet, Ms
Supervisor: Goldstein, Harvey, Prof. (Project Director) |

Screening and special educational provision in schools project.

Background: This project aims to investigate different methods of identification and provision for children with special educational needs in the ordinary school; the focus is on the child who does not need a statement, i.e. 'Warnock's 18%'. The identification of these children is largely through teacher referral with the help of standardized tests and/or checklists, and recently there has been an increasing use of curriculum-related learning objectives and classroom-based assessments. Factors such as the 1981 Education Act, cuts in educational expenditure and changing views about effective models of SEN support mean that many LEA services are either changing or planning change. There is a growing consensus that the most efficient use of resources is to give advice and support to classroom teachers in identifying and helping the SEN child within the normal classroom. The project aims to investigate the implications of this policy for teachers and children and also to collect information on effective resource allocation with the intention of developing a possible model to assist LEAs systematize their allocation procedures.

Design: The research has a progressively narrowing focus. At national level a questionnaire survey has already collected basic information on screening programmes, other methods of identification and provision in LEAs in England and Wales. At local level, six LEAs will be studied in detail using interviews and study of documents to illustrate differing styles of practice. Interviews and observation techniques will then be employed to investigate identification and provision at school level, thereby determining any mismatch between LEA policy and school practice.

Date of Research: March 1983–February 1986.

Published Material: GIPPS, C. and GROSS, H. (1984). Local Education Authority policies for identification and provision for children with special educational needs in ordinary schools. Results of a national questionnaire survey carried out in the Autumn of 1983.
UNPUBLISHED series of Occasional Papers:
GIPPS, C. and GOLDSTEIN, H. Local and national testing in the UK: the last ten years. Paper presented at the conference of American Educational Research Association, Easter 1984.
GIPPS, C. and GOLDSTEIN, H. Twenty per cent with special educational needs; another legacy from Cyril Burt? May 1984.

KEYWORDS: screening; remediation; Education Act 1981; assessment; educational
provision; policy

1/087   MRC/London University Institute of   Montgomery, Diane, Ms (Faculty
             Education   of Education, Kingston
             Bedford Way   Polytechnic)
             London WC1 0AL   Supervisor: Frith, Uta, Dr
             Tel: 01-636-1500

An investigation of articulation accessing in spelling disability.

Background: A close association has been found between the ability to blend and
manipulate phonemes and reading achievement over the last 20 years (Chall, 1963;
Liberman, 1973; Calfee, 1973; Bryant and Bradley, 1978; Snowling, 1981). Pupils with
severe reading disability also most often have severe spelling problems (Miles, 1983), but
the reverse is not always true (Frith, 1981). It was hypothesized that although spelling
disability was associated with difficulties and disabilities in phoneme segmentation there
was not necessarily a causative relationship. A third factor, articulation accessing
difficulty, was proposed as the origin of both spelling and phoneme segmentation
problems.
Design: A series of experiments were undertaken presenting phoneme segmentation and
articulation accessing tests to groups of subjects with severe spelling and reading
retardation ('dyslexics') of at least two years decrement, and control subjects.
Size: The groups were matched for reading age at around eight years but of different
chronological age (ten and eight years) and intelligence. In all, data from 138 'dyslexics'
and 72 control subjects were analysed.
Methods: The data were subject to correlational tests and analysis of variance and
covariance revealing significantly poorer performance of 'dyslexic' subjects on articulation accessing ($p < 01$) but not on phoneme segmentation after a reading age of eight had
been attained.

Results: The poor spellers all showed signs of previous articulation accessing difficulty
and conclusions were drawn with respect to both early screening and remedial education
advocating multi-sensory mouth training. Changes in theoretical paradigms were
proposed suggesting a new origin of 'dyslexia'.

Date of Research: April 1979 – April 1984.

Published Material: MONTGOMERY, D. (1981). 'Do Dyslexics have Difficulty
Accessing Articulatory Information?' *Psychological Research*, **43,** pp. 235 – 243.
MONTGOMERY, D. (Ed.) (1984). *Teaching Reading Through Spelling Vol 2: The
Foundations of the Programme.* (Learning difficulties project, Kingston Polytechnic).

KEYWORDS: articulation accessing; spelling disability; dyslexia; phonemic processing;
reading; primary

1/088   Thomas Coram Research Unit   Bowler, Dermot
             University of London Institute of   Supervisor: Kiernan, C.C., Prof.
             Education   (currently at Hester Adrian
             41, Brunswick Square   Research Centre, Manchester
             London WC1N 1AZ   University)
             Tel: 01-278-2424

Modality differences in short-term memory of severely mentally handicapped children.

Background: Manual sign systems have been used successfully to help severely mentally handicapped subjects to communicate (Kiernan, Reid and Jones, 1982). Work carried out by O'Connor and Hermelin (1978) on auditory and visual sequencing in this population showed a preference for visual and spatial organization of information.

Design: The present series of studies was designed to test empirically the conceptual parallels which can be drawn between these two lines of research as well as to explore handicapped children's handling of referential and non-referential signs and words in short-term memory.

Size: The investigation is being carried out on a sample of 20 severely retarded children with a mean Peabody MA of 64 months.

Methods: All subjects were taught sign or word names for a set of 20 cartoon pictures. Experiment I. I examined short-term memory for single items by presenting a sign or word and asking the child to identify the appropriate referent items after a delay of 1, 5 or 10 seconds.
Experiment II was similar to Experiment I with the addition of a task in the delay interval to prevent rehearsal.
Experiments III and IV examined children's handling of strings of four signs or words.

Results: The data are not, as yet, fully analysed, but preliminary analyses suggest that there are marked individual preferences for one or other modality, which are reasonably stable across tasks and measures.

Date of Research: PhD thesis, started part-time in October 1977. Hope to complete by October 1985.

Published Material: KIERNAN, C.C., REID, B.D. and JONES, L.M. (1982). *Signs and Symbols: A Review of Literature and Survey of the Use of Non-Vocal Communication Systems.* University of London Institute of Education Studies in Education, No. 11. London: Heinemann.
O'CONNOR, N. and HERMELIN, B. (1978). *Seeing and Hearing and Space and Time.* New York: Academic Press.
BOWLER, D.M. (1984). Short term memory strategies for verbal and manual sign labels used by mentally handicapped children. In: BERG, J.M. (Ed) *Perspectives and Progress in Mental Retardation, Volume 1, Social, Psychological and Educational aspects.* Baltimore Md.: University Park Press. pp. 229–238.

KEYWORDS: short-term memory; mental handicap; manual sign language.

1/089   Thomas Coram Research Unit   Kiernan, C.C., Prof. (currently at
              University of London Institute of   Hester Adrian Research Centre,
              Education   Manchester University); Bowler,
              41, Brunswick Square   Dermot; Reid, Barbara, Ms
              London WC1N 1AZ
              Tel: 01-278-2424

Diagnostic techniques in relation to the teaching of speech signs and symbols.

Background: The growth of use of augmentative systems (sign languages and symbol systems) with mentally handicapped individuals has highlighted problems of understanding and facilitating early communication skills. The project was aimed at producing assessment procedures which could be used to aid programme placement and development.

Design: Several assessment procedures were explored, including report and observation methods, visual hemifield and dichotic listening procedures.

Size: In each case pilot procedures were devised and several of the procedures were further standardized.

Methods: Inter-observer reliabilities were established for questionnaire procedures and test–retest reliabilities for test procedures. Experimental procedures were cross-validated.

Results: Several procedures were developed, in particular a Pre-verbal Communication Schedule (PVC) and an Environmental Assessment, and experimental procedures were developed to cover dichotic listening and visual hemifield procedures.

Date of Research: September 1980–January 1984.

KEYWORDS: *mental handicap; communication; sign language; speech; graphic symbol; assessment.*

1/090   Thomas Coram Research Unit   *Supervisor:* Kiernan, C.C., Prof.
         University of London Institute of   (currently at Hester Adrian
         Education   Research Centre, Manchester
         41, Brunswick Square   University)
         London WC1N 1AZ
         Tel: 01-278-2424

The acquisition and recall of spoken words and manual signs by mentally handicapped children.

Background: Since the early 1970s, manual sign language has been successfully used with many severely handicapped children who have failed to develop speech. Although several clinical reports have been published, the literature contained little experimental work on the cognitive processing of signs relative to spoken words for this population. This thesis describes a series of eight such experiments, four on acquisition and four on recall.

Design: Experiments one to four explored sign-word differences in acquisition. The second and third experiments further explored this facilitative effect, adding two controls for motivational factors. Experiments five to eight compared recall of signs and words (or, in experiment seven, words taken from different taxonomic categories).

Results: Taken together, the series of eight experiments showed an advantage for manual signs over spoken words on rate of acquisition, same facilitation of word-learning by previous sign-learning, and a slight advantage for spoken words over manual signs in recall.

Date of Research: September 1976–August 1984.

Published Material: REID, B.D. and KIERNAN, C.C. (1979). 'Spoken words and manual signs as encoding categories in short-term memory for mentally retarded children; *American Journal of Mental Deficiency*, **84**, 2, 200–203.
REID, B.D. (1984). 'The acquisition and recall of signs and words by mentally handicapped children. In: Berg, J. & De JONG, J. (Eds) *Perspectives and Progress in Mental Retardation Vol 1*, Proceedings of the Sixth Congress of the International Association for the Scientific Study of Mental Deficiency, Toronto, Baltimore: University Park Press.

KEYWORDS: *manual sign language; coding; mental handicap; cognitive processing; signing system.*

1/091   Department of Child and Adolescent   Taylor, Eric, Dr; Sandberg, Seija,
             Psychiatry   Dr
             University of London Institute of
             Psychiatry
             De Crespigny Park
             Denmark Hill
             London SE5 8AF
             Tel. 01-703-5411

Survey of hyperactive boys in ordinary primary and special schools.

Background: Hyperactivity is infrequently recognized as a specific problem in the UK. This study aims to examine the nature and significance of hyperactive behaviour and its distinction from other syndromes of disturbed conduct.

Design: Comparison of hyperactive children, with and without conduct disorder, with children showing pure syndromes of conduct disorder and inattention, and with normal controls.

Size: 4,000 boys aged six and seven years in a London Borough's schools.

Methods: Screening with parents' and teachers' questionnaires to establish comparison groups, followed by intensive psychological, psychiatric and neurological measures applied to those groups.

Results: Preliminary results suggest hyperactivity to be a distinct pattern of disordered behaviour, associated with other kinds of developmental delay.

Date of Research: July 1981–March 1985.

KEYWORDS: *hyperactivity; attention deficit; epidemiology; conduct disorder; screening; assessment.*

1/092   MRC Social Psychiatry Unit   Shah, Amitta, Ms
             University of London Institute of   *Supervisors:* Frith, Uta, Dr; Wing,
             Psychiatry   Lorna, Dr
             De Crespigny Park
             London SE5
             Tel. 01-703-5411 ext. 328

The nature of cognitive processing on visuo-spatial tasks in young autistic adults and a comparison group of non-autistic people.

Background: Autistic children's performance on certain cognitive tasks is at a much higher level than on others. These 'peaks' have been generally noted on the block design and object assembly tests of the Wechsler scales and have been broadly referred to as 'visuo-spatial' skills. However, it is not clear what particular cognitive ability (or strategy) this refers to as the tasks involve a variety of spatial, cognitive and perceptual skills. The overall aim is to investigate this phenomenon and work out the precise nature of these so called 'visuo-spatial' skills. The basic questions asked are how do autistic people do these spatial tasks, what are they and how do these differ from strategies used by non-autistic people?

Design: The question is tackled by breaking down these complex tasks into their various components and examining how information is processed at each level using experimental psychology techniques.

Size: Twenty autistic people aged between 16 and 25; 20 non-autistic people aged between 16 and 25 and matched with the autistic subjects on overall cognitive ability.

Methods: So far experimental methods have been used to look at specific spatial abilities such as location of spatial position with and without additional contextual cues, construction of spatial designs of varying difficulty and requiring varying components of visuo-constructional skill; mental rotation ability has been investigated using a micro-computer to run the experiment and to collect the data. This has been very successful with autistic people.

Date of Research: January 1983–December 1985 (estimated).

KEYWORDS: *autistic; visuo-spatial skills; cognitive processing; spatial location; adult.*

Manchester University

1/093   Department of Audiology &   Lynas, Wendy, Miss
               Education of the Deaf
               University of Manchester
               Manchester M13 9PL
               Tel. 061-273-3333

Aspects of the integration of hearing impaired pupils in ordinary schools.

Background: To get a better understanding of the situation which occurs when severely and profoundly deaf children are placed alongside normally hearing ones in ordinary classrooms. The study focuses on the perspectives of the ordinary class teacher, normally hearing pupil and hearing impaired pupil.
Design: 1978–79: Observation and interviewing in ordinary schools.
1983–84: Follow-up interviews of hearing impaired youngsters to get longitudinal dimension.
Size: Study involved observing and interviewing 50 hearing impaired pupils, 40 approx. class teachers and 40 approx. (interviews) normally hearing pupils.
Methods: Qualitative – Classroom observation
               Informal interviews.

Date of Research: 1978–Summer 1985.

KEYWORDS: *integration; hearing impairment; longitudinal*

1/094   Department of Audiology and   Rooke, Philippa, Miss (Dept. of
               Education of the Deaf   Linguistics, Sheffield University)
               University of Manchester   *Supervisors:* McCartney, Elspeth,
               Oxford Road   Ms; Cullen, Chris, Dr (Swinton
               Manchester M13 9PL   Hospital, Manchester)
               Tel. 061-273-3333

A structured teaching programme for the profoundly retarded multiply handicapped based on certain principles of Conductive Education.

Background: Conductive Education is a system of education, developed in Hungary by Dr Andras Petö, for motorically handicapped people of normal intelligence. It has been used in Britain with a wide range of client groups, including the mentally handicapped. The aim of the research project was to evaluate the effectiveness, if any, of Conductive Education for mentally handicapped children.
Design: The project was set up in one special school in the West Midlands and compared the achievements of a group of children receiving one hour per day of Conductive

Education with a second group, the control group, who followed a more traditional teaching approach throughout the day.

Size: The sample consisted of ten children; five in the experimental group and five in the control group.

Methods: An assessment schedule was designed specifically for the project. The children were tested every six to eight weeks using this schedule, and in addition a questionnaire was given to each staff member at the end of the project. The results indicated that the children in the experimental group made no more progress than the controls. Conductive Education, therefore, is not an effective method of teaching for profoundly retarded multiply handicapped children. Teacher attitude was an interesting aspect of the study and it is suggested that this could be an important dependent variable in future research with this population.

Date of Research: March 1981 – December 1983.

Published Material: ROOKE, P. (1983). 'A cross-disciplinary approach to teaching the profoundly retarded multiply handicapped, using speech as a regulator of behaviour'. In: *Proceedings of the 14th Congress of the International Association of Logopaedics and Phoniatrics, Edinburgh, August 1983.*
ROOKE, P. and OPEN, P. (1983). 'An approach to teaching profoundly retarded multiply handicapped children based on certain principles of Conductive Education', *Mental Handicap* (formerly *Apex*) **11,** 73 – 75.

KEYWORDS: conductive education; mental handicap; multiple handicap; teacher attitude.

1/095   Department of Educational Guidance   Edmonds, Marie, Ms
             University of Manchester   *Supervisor:* Farrell, Peter
             Oxford Road
             Manchester M13 9PL
             Tel. 061-273-3333

The maintenance of skills in teachers of the severely mentally handicapped, following an EDY course in behavioural techniques.

Background: To evaluate the maintenance and generalization of skills acquired by teachers who attended an EDY Behaviour Modification Course. It was the extension of a research project carried out by Judith McBrien (1982).

Design: A non-equivalent two group design was used. All the teachers were pre-tested using a behavioural skill assessment form and then one group of four teachers from one school trained using the EDY course. Both groups were post-tested at the end of the course, with a further test one year later. The four teachers who underwent the training course were also observed after one year in the classroom situation.

Size: Two groups of four teachers in two schools for the severely mentally handicapped were involved in the study. The background and training of the teachers were similar. They were all volunteers and each group included the Deputy Head.

Methods: All pre- post- and classroom tests were video-taped (28) and rated 'blind' by two independent raters. The data was subjected to a two-way analysis of variance. A test of theoretical knowledge of behavioural terminology and skills which accompanied the EDY course was readministered to the four trained teachers at the end of the course and at one year follow-up.

Results: Suggested that teachers can acquire behavioural skills following an EDY course and that performance is maintained over time and generalized to classroom situation. Evidence from the teachers' theoretical knowledge test did not support the hypothesis that there is a relationship between theoretical knowledge and practical ability.

Date of Research: January 1983–September 1983.

Published Material: McBRIEN, J. (1982). An Evaluation of a Training Course in Behavioural Techniques for Staff Working with Severely Mentally Handicapped Children. Unpublished dissertation, University of Manchester.

KEYWORDS: EDY course; in-service education; behaviour modification; mental handicap; teacher training; severe learning difficulties

---

1/096   Department of Education   Lonton, A.P.
             University of Manchester
             Oxford Road
             Manchester MI3 9PL
             Tel: 061-273-3333 ext. 3603

Educational, social and neuropsychological studies of adults & children with spina bifida, hydrocephalus & related problems.

Background: Sheffield Children's Hospital has the world's largest and best known clinic for treating spina bifida, hydrocephalus and related problems. The psychologist is one of the specialists in the multidisciplinary team which assesses and treats these children.
Design: Research is based on hospital clinical data, and is directed at whatever topic is seen to be most important or worthy of investigation. Much of the work has been directed at correlating neurological abnormalities with educational, psychological and physical outcomes, e.g. lacunar skull deformities & intelligence; location of the spina bifida & intellectual skills; thickness of cortex & intelligence; prediction of intelligence in neonates. Some studies have evaluated new treatments, e.g. the use of isosorbide for hydrocephalus. Other research has been directed at the problems of SB adults.
Size: The sample includes: 1,243 spina bifida patients; 263 congenital hydrocephalics; 159 with acquired hydrocephalus; 97 encephaloceles; 87 lipomas; and 150 with large heads but not hydrocephalics. Mean age of group is 18 years, but sample includes ages from birth to 26 years.
Methods: Psychometric, educational and medical data have been intercorrelated by means of standard statistical packages used on the computerized data bank.

Results: Among the results have been indications of the prognostic values of lacunar skull deformities, lesion location, thickness of cortex, and the type of neural tube malformation with respect to the physical and intellectual functioning of children with spina bifida. The social class structure and relevance of class to psychological and educational functioning have been studied. Abnormalities of hand preference have been found, particularly in children with higher lesions. The integration of these children in ordinary schools has been fostered since 1975, and the results evaluated. In recent years attention has been directed towards the needs and service requirements for adults with spina bifida.

Date of Research: Started May 1973–Ongoing.

KEYWORDS: spina bifida; hydrocephalus; integration; neurology; adult; physical handicap

---

1/097   Department of Education   Tobin, David
             University of Manchester   *Supervisor:* Mittler, P., Prof.;
             Oxford Road   Farrell, P.
             Manchester MI3 9PL
             Tel: 061-273-3333

The maintenance of behaviour change in children with severe mental handicap.

Background: Only 12 per cent of studies published in behavioural journals report follow-up data of more than six months duration. Serious questions must be raised regarding the outcome of behavioural interventions. This therefore is a critical issue in the field of mental handicap.

The aim of this research is to discover what treatment effects, if any, are in evidence several months after treatment programmes have been terminated. A further aim is to identify those strategies which are more successful in maintaining behaviour change.

Design: It is proposed that two groups of pupils who are mentally handicapped will be followed-up. Group 1 (18 pupils) will receive a treatment programme for a problem behaviour or skill deficiency but no specific maintenance programmes will be devised. Group 2 will follow the same procedure as Group 1 but in addition a very specific maintenance strategy will be devised. Both groups will be followed-up several months after the termination of the programmes.

Size: Group 1:18 pupils; Group 2:16 pupils, Total 34 pupils.

Problem Behaviours – poor attention, out of seat behaviour, non-compliance.

Skill Deficiencies – eye contact, visual discrimination, motor skills, language.

Methods: Observation by student teachers and class teachers. Inter-rater reliability checks by students not directly concerned with the study or the pupils – such observers unaware of the groups to which pupils belong:

Salient factors in programming maintenance.

The role of reinforcement in teaching and natural settings.

The selection of agents of control.

The choice of target behaviours.

Date of Research: January 1984 – June 1989.

KEYWORDS: follow-up study; behaviour change; severe learning difficulties; mental handicap; behaviour problem; skill deficiency

1/098   Department of Education   Yates, Jeffrey
              University of Manchester   *Supervisor:* Elliott, Colin, Dr
              Oxford Road
              Manchester MI3 9PL
              Tel: 061-273-3333

The impact of manual sign acquisition on communication in language, handicapped, severely retarded, autistic and sociable children.

Background: Various attempts have been made to teach manual signs to autistic and mentally retarded children but few have considered the pre-existing communicative repertoires and social interaction patterns of the individuals involved.

This study aims to compare and contrast such interactions and communicative skills in two groups of mentally retarded, severely language handicapped children, one group autistic and the other sociable, and to assess the differential impact of teaching manual signs on communication in such children.

Design: An initial teaching lexicon of manual signs was compiled using research into expressive language development. The lexical items were translated into British Sign Language (BSL) signs by a native signer. The items were rated for translucency (iconicity) and motor-complexity using experimental techniques.

Size: Twelve children.

Methods: The items were taught in an order determined by indices of high iconicity and low complexity and by individual communicative needs, to two groups of children, six sociable and six autistic. The impact on communicative skills was assessed.

Results: The study is still ongoing but preliminary results suggest that autism/sociability is a major factor in the acquisition and use of signs and that communication is a product of social interaction rather than the availability of a symbolic system for coding communicative exchanges.

Date of Research: October 1981 – December 1984.

KEYWORDS: autism; non-verbal communication; mental handicap; British sign language; signing system

1/099   Hester Adrian Research Centre   Robson, Colin, Dr; Sebba, Judy,
             University of Manchester   Ms
             Oxford Road   *Supervisors:* Robson, C., Dr
             Manchester MI3 9PL   (Huddersfield Poly/HARC);
             Tel: 061-273-3333 ext. 3500 or 3508   Sebba, J., Ms (HARC); Mittler,
                                                    P., Prof., (Education Dept.,
                                                    Manchester University) (Project
                                                    co-directors)

Project Impact: In-service education and special educational needs

Background: This project is concerned with the extent to which skills and knowledge acquired on in-service courses in special education are put into practice in the classroom. The research is set within the context of an innovatory regional modular course currently being developed, which will lead to an advanced specialist qualification in special educational needs. Continuous evaluation of the modular scheme will assist change and development and extend the range of units offered to the participants.

Design: Teacher training has sometimes suffered from a lack of integration between theory and practice. The modular scheme attempts to overcome this problem by having a compulsory school-focussed element involving classroom or school-based activities as part of the course. The effectiveness of these courses will be investigated through case studies of course models and by evaluating the impact of developed courses. The project will also be concerned with exploring some of the organizational factors which determine schools' receptivity to change. Throughout the project, information on the working of the regional course will be disseminated. It is intended to generate training packs from some of the courses involved in the scheme.

Methods: Questionaire; interviews; classroom and school observation; non-participant observation of courses.

Date of Research: October 1983 – September 1986.

KEYWORDS: school-focussed training; training pack; in-service education; behavioural teaching approach

Mayfield Computer Dyslexia Group

1/100   Bradley House   Brother Henry
             Little Trodgers Lane
             Mayfield
             E. Sussex TN20 6PW

Computer aids in the adult literacy field.

Background: The investigation into the problems of adult illiterates arose out of our efforts to help dyslexics. The problems are in some respects similar, but are exacerbated by psychological problems due to age. There is more emphasis on recognizing common words in social usage (up, exit, private) etc. and on recognizing road traffic signs and being able to fill in forms and write legibly, than in mastering a really extensive vocabulary.

Design: Two computers were fixed on for the programs – the BBC model B for its excellent graphics, and colour, and the Spectrum for its graphics, colour and, above all, price. Some Adult Literacy Groups have chosen one, some the other, but the point must be made that three Spectrums can be bought for the price of one BBC.

Methods: Frequent consultation with teachers in this field, and sessions with students themselves. This involves not only the supervisor but boys and girls of Mayfield College and St Leonards School who form the team of programmers, and we find this procedure motivates the team very well.

As in the dyslexia programs, a small copying fee is charged to enable us to stay abreast of developments. Programs will be available on tape and disc for the two machines mentioned, and also if desired on the Microdrive for the Spectrum.

Date of Research: December 1983–Ongoing.

KEYWORDS: microcomputer; software; adult literacy

1/101   Bradley House   Brother Henry
               Little Trodgers Lane
               Mayfield
               E. Sussex TN20 6PW

The use of microcomputers to aid dyslexics.

Background: Dyslexia afflicts up to ten per cent of the male population – up to two per cent of females. The microcomputer can help dyslexics to help themselves; it relaxes them, and twice as many pupils can be engaged as before.

Spelling, an important, but not the only aspect of dyslexia, can be taught with data-type programs, in which vocabularies can be altered by teachers.

Special programs for helping left/right confusion, telling the time, and direction and bearings can be very effective.

Design: 1. To devise diagnostic programs to alert teachers to the need for assessment.
2. To provide structured programs to aid:
(a) Spelling;
(b) Left/right confusion and its associated problems, map-reading, telling the way, etc.;
(c) Short term memory;
(d) To give aid to writing, which is often bad in dyslexics.

Methods: Consultation with dyslexia teachers, and feedback from them. Exhibition at conferences, and user groups. The programs are in a large part devised and produced by senior pupils of Mayfield College, and St Leonards-Mayfield School. They are all in the public domain, but a small charge is made for copying.

Computers covered are Commodore PET and 64, RM380Z (disc only), BBC (tape or disc), Sinclair Spectrum (tape, microdrive, and, shortly, disc). The RM380Z programs will also run on 480Z machines and we think that the BBC programs will also run on the Acorn Electron.

Results: Schools and resource centres all over the country are using programs, but the desired feedback is, with a few honourable exceptions, much less than could be desired.

Date of Research: October 1979–Ongoing.

Published Material: 27 programs on tape or disc (obtainable from source). A book to show teachers how programs may be altered to suit their own local conditions is in course of preparation.

KEYWORDS: *short-term memory; dyslexia; microcomputer; software; spelling*

Medical Research Council

1/102   MRC Cognitive Development Unit   Baron-Cohen, Simon
             17 Gordon Street   *Supervisor:* Frith, Uta, Dr
             London WC1

An investigation of autistic children's social understanding.

Background: To investigate if autistic children can represent what another person is thinking/believing.

Design: Experimental paradigms included a puppet story, and a *picture-sequencing task.* Performance of control groups matched on mental age (verbal and non-verbal) and chronological age was tested.

Size: Control groups included Down's Syndrome children and normal children.

Results: Autistic children, although of a higher MA and IQ and CA than Down's syndrome subjects, performed significantly worse than either of the control groups on both social cognition tasks.

Date of Research: October 1983 – October 1984.

KEYWORDS: *autistic; social cognition; Down's syndrome*

Meldreth Manor School

1/103   Meldreth Manor School   Martin, Andrew
             Fenny Lane   *Supervisors:* Devereux, K., Mrs
             Meldreth   (Cambridge Institute of Education
             Royston   and Meldreth Manor School)
             Herts. SG8 6LG
             Tel: 0763-60771

An evaluation of the use of computer programs in teaching counting skills to multiply handicapped pupils.

Background: The aim of the project is to assess the effectiveness of using computer programs to teach counting skills to multiply handicapped pupils. It involves the use of the computer as an enabling device to allow physically handicapped pupils to count objects on screen by use of switches.

Design: The pupils were tested on their ability to count and recognize groups of up to five coloured cubes and pictures. The test was repeated after one week. They will work for a short period each day on a structured series of computer programs and scores will be kept. At the end of the threshold period the pre-test will be repeated.

Size: The subjects of the study are five students in the 16+ – age group, all of whom suffer from physical handicaps which greatly limit their ability to manipulate objects, as well as being mentally handicapped.

Date of Research: March 1984–October 1984.

KEYWORDS: computer; multiple handicap; physical handicap; numeracy; counting; computer assisted learning

1/104   Psychology and Research   Purushothaman, Madhavan
              Department
              Meldreth Manor School
              Fenny Lane
              Meldreth
              Royston
              Herts. SG8 6LG
              Tel: 0763-60771/5

To establish a data base on the development and progress of cerebral palsied children with severe mental and physical disabilities

Background: Currently children are assessed, on admission, with an in-house document called Progress and Information Schedule (PIS). This is a very detailed assessment, taking a minimum of three months to a maximum of a year, during which the child's special needs are identified and recommendations are made on appropriate intervention programmes to meet the identified needs. Although the child's progress is monitored from time to time, and certainly on an annual basis, there are no systematic procedures for assessing the reliability and validity of the initial assessment and recommendations, and there has been no attempt to look at development from a theoretical (say deficit/difference) model. The main aims are, therefore, (i) to examine the validity of initial assessment and (ii) to investigate the nature and type of development.

Design: Record the child's levels of functioning in the following areas: language and communication; feeding; mobility; discrimination skills; social and emotional development; self-help skills; imitation; interests; and other cognitive skills as appropriate and as assessed by PIS. Record the levels again at 'critical' points when recommended programmes are completed.

Size: The aim is to generate hypotheses rather than attempt to test any. Hope to follow up all the children who are admitted to the school from April 1984 until April 1985 when the position will be reviewed.

Methods: Each child's level of functioning will be recorded on video tapes initially, and then at each criticial point such as the completion of an individualized programme, transfer from one class to another or from one house to another. Ratings will be made or tests administered as appropriate and progress assessed in an 'illuminative style'.

Date of Research: April 1984–December 1987.

KEYWORDS: cerebral palsy; multiple handicap; longitudinal; assessment

Mid-Kent College

| 1/105 | Department of Management and
Social Work Studies
Mid-Kent College
Maidstone Road
Chatham
Kent
Tel: 0634-41001 | Akhurst, Colin R.
Supervisor: Picardie, Michael
(Dept. of Social Administration,
University College, Cardiff) |

The life-styles of families with a handicapped child.

Background: The study seeks to test conceptual models of family response to the presence of a handicapped child. Aiming to strengthen the foundations of social work practices with such families.
Size: Forty volunteer families.
Methods: Mainly using extensive interviews following a schedule, but also questionnaires and repertory grids.

Results: Not completed at this stage.

Date of Research: 1979–Due 1985.

KEYWORDS: life-style; family; social work

Moray House College of Education, Edinburgh

| 1/106 | Special Education Department
Moray House College of Education
Holyrood Road
Edinburgh
Tel: 031-556-8455 | Watson, Judith, Dr |

Special educational provision for young children with communication difficulties.

Background: The proposal is to investigate the nature and effect of specialized educational provision for young children of normal intellectual ability to cope with ordinary primary school.
Design: (1) Follow-up information on pupils' educational & social progress. (2) Information on family background and parents. (3) Naturalistic observation and recording of dialogue in different settings.
Size: Approximately 25–30 children in attendance at language units.
Methods: (1) Information obtained from records. (2) Information obtained from structured interviews. (3) Information received from target children by radiomicrophone.

Date of Research: October 1983–October 1987(?).

KEYWORDS: communication difficulties; language unit; programme evaluation; parents

Muscular Dystrophy Group of Great Britain and Northern Ireland

1/107   17 Selby Road
Plaistow
London E13 8NB

Cordes, Wilfred, (Chairman
Welfare Committee)

Muscular dystrophy survey.

Background: The Muscular Dystrophy Group of Great Britain and Northern Ireland is primarily concerned with the advancement of medical research into Neuromuscular Diseases. Some ten years ago the Group's Welfare Committee was formed to provide information and support to patients and their parents. This Survey is an attempt to obtain information about the school, post school and employment experiences of Muscular Dystrophy sufferers. It is hoped that patterns of experience will emerge which will indicate a relationship between the degree of disability, the choice of educational options and attainments and employment prospects.

Design: The questionnaire is in two parts:

Factual Information	*Comments about Experiences.*
Type of School	Choice of School
Educational Attainments	Access
Further/Higher Educational	Transport
attainments	Support services
(Qualifications obtained)	
Employment	
Day centres	

Size: The questionnaires were distributed throughout Great Britain and Northern Ireland by Family Care Officers based at our major medical centres, through some 500 local branches and representatives of the Group and 50 special P.H. schools situated outside areas covered by the branches.

Methods: Questionnaires

Results: When the Survey is concluded I shall present summaries of the material received to the Welfare Committee, together with a separate section detailing my personal comments and conclusions to stimulate discussion regarding the uses to which the knowledge gained can be put.

Date of Research: June 1983 – December 1984 (Approx.).

KEYWORDS: muscular dystrophy; further education; higher education; employment

National Bureau for Handicapped Students

1/108   National Bureau for Handicapped
Students
40 Brunswick Square
London WC 1N 1AZ

Cooper, Deborah, Ms; Stowell,
Richard

Provision for handicapped students in the member states of the EEC.

Background: To investigate post-compulsory education and training provision for young people with special needs in the member states of the EEC.

Design: Investigation of opportunities and facilities for young people (14–25) in education and training in the ten member states of the EEC.
Methods: Review of literature; discussions with professionals, voluntary groups, handicapped people; visits to examples of good practice.

Date of Research: January 1984–November 1984.

KEYWORDS: educational provision; adult; further education; training; EEC; post-16

| 1/109 | National Bureau for Handicapped Students 40 Brunswick Square London WC 1N 1AZ | Williams, Gwilym |

The training needs of further education lecturers teaching handicapped students.

Background: To investigate the existing training and qualifications of FE lecturers teaching handicapped students, and their attitude towards and need for further training.
Design: A postal survey of FE lecturers teaching handicapped students.
Size: 200 FE colleges and 330 individual lecturers.
Methods: A postal questionnaire survey.

Date of Research: 1981–December 1984.

KEYWORDS: further education; training; needs survey

National Centre for Down's Syndrome
see under Birmingham Polytechnic

National Elfrida Rathbone Society

| 1/110 | National Elfrida Rathbone Society Room 22 Unit 15, The Arches Industrial Estate Spon End Coventry CV1 3JQ Tel: 0203-74575 | Telford, Jean, Mrs |

Investigation into the post-school activities of leavers from four special schools in Coventry.

Background: (i) To gain information about educationally handicapped school leavers in Coventry (ii) To influence decision makers such as Careers Office, Schools, MSC, Education Department to do more for the educatonally handicapped, such as setting up a YTS Scheme for special school leavers.
Design: Interviews with a random sample of special school leavers which will be used as the basis for a detailed report on their post school activities and needs.
Size: Random sample comprising approximately 20 per cent of special school leavers 1979–1983 inclusive.

Methods: Personal interview at subject's home, researcher completing questionnaire.

Date of Research: November 1983–October 1984.

KEYWORDS: school leaver; transition to adult life; employment; ESN(M); Youth Training Scheme.

National Foundation for Educational Research

1/111   National Foundation for Educational   Bradley, Judy, Dr
              Research   *Supervisor:* Hegarty, Seamus, Dr
              The Mere   (Special Needs)
              Upton Park
              Slough
              Berks. SL1 2DQ
              Tel: 0735-74123

Evaluation of dissemination and take-up of RP 138 resource back.

Background: A staff development resource pack for FE teachers of students with moderate learning difficulties has been produced by NFER (see entry No. 1/112) and is being disseminated throughout 1985 through a number of regional conferences. This project is monitoring the take-up and evaluating the use made of the pack.
Design: An action study to stimulate the take-up of the pack while at the same time examining the dissemination process in a more general way, monitoring the reception given to the pack and evaluating the use made of it at the regional and local levels.
Methods: Questionnaires, interviews, group discussion meetings, observation.

Date of Research: October 1984–March 1986.

KEYWORDS: further education; staff development; moderate learning difficulties; dissemination; in-service education.

1/112   National Foundation for Educational   Bradley, Judy, Dr
              Research   *Supervisor:* Hegarty, Seamus, Dr
              The Mere   (Special Needs)
              Upton Park
              Slough
              Berks. SL1 2DQ
              Tel: 0735-74123

Staff development resource pack for FE teachers of students with moderate learning difficulties.

Background: Young people with moderate learning difficulties represent a new student group in further education. The aim of the project was to produce a multi-media staff development resource pack designed to make a significant contribution to the professional development of all those involved in the further eduction and training of these students.
Design: Collection of materials for use in the pack from a wide range of colleges currently providing for this student group.

Methods: Field visits involving interviewing, observation and collection of original material on college provision for students with moderate learning difficulties.

Results: Written up in the form of staff development pack for use by FE teachers.

Date of Research: April 1983–September 1984.

Published Material: BRADLEY, J. *et al.* (1985). *From Coping to Confidence: A Staff Development Resource Pack for FE Teachers of Students with Moderate Learning Difficulties.* Available from Editorial Services, NFER, The Mere, Upton Park, Slough SL1 2DQ.

KEYWORDS: further education; staff development; moderate learning difficulties; videotape; inservice education.

1/113   National Foundation for Educational   Dean, Alan
             Research   *Supervisor:* Hegarty, Seamus, Dr
             The Mere   (Special Needs)
             Upton Park
             Slough
             Berks. SL1 2DQ
             Tel: 0735-74123

Provision for students with severe learning difficulties.

Background: 1) To carry out a survey of local authority provision within further and adult education for students with severe learning difficulties. 2) To observe significant issues in these forms of provision, and detail examples of good practice.
Design: 1) A survey of provision in colleges of further and adult education throughout England and Wales. 2) Commissioned papers which discuss important issues, and others which detail current practices.
Size: All colleges of further and adult education which make appropriate provision.
Methods: Postal survey and edited papers from external authors.

Date of Research: April 1984–October 1984.

Published Material: DEAN, A. and HEGARTY, S. (Eds) (1984). *Learning for Independence: post-16 educational provision for people with severe learning difficulties.* London: FEU.

KEYWORDS: post-16; further education; adult education; severe learning difficulties

1/114   National Foundation for Educational   Dee, Lesley, Ms
             Research   *Supervisor:* Hegarty, Seamus, Dr
             The Mere   (Special Needs)
             Upton Park
             Slough
             Berks. SL1 2DQ
             Tel: 0735-74123

A curriculum framework for students with severe learning difficulties in FE.

Background: The aims of the project are:
(i) to develop a curriculum framework for young people aged 16–19 with severe learning difficulties; (ii) to explore its implementation within an FE setting; (iii) to evaluate and to document the process of constructing and effecting such a framework.

This project complements the review of post-16 provision commissioned and published by the FEU in Autumn 1984, *Learning for Independence.*

Design: The project is divided into three phases. The first two are based in eight colleges and units in Somerset and Devon which run courses for students with severe learning difficulties. During this period a curriculum framework with accompanying materials, teaching methods and assessment tools will be generated by the project team. Phase III, which will last 12 months, extends into selected LEAs and institutions wishing to be involved in piloting and evaluating the curriculum framework.

Methods: The principal approach is that of action research supported by interview, observation, case-study questionnaires and small-scale surveys. In addition three residential seminars will be held.

Results: A report suitable for publication by FEU which will:
(i) describe a curriculum framework; (ii) describe and evaluate the curriculum development process; (iii) provide materials and assessment instruments. This will be disseminated via one or more short courses or conferences.

Date of Research: September 1984–August 1986.

KEYWORDS: curriculum development; severe learning difficulties; further education; post-16; curriculum framework

1/115   National Foundation for Educational   Hodgson, A., Dr; Hegarty,
              Research   Seamus, Dr
              The Mere
              Upton Park
              Slough
              Berks. SL1 2DQ
              Tel: 0735-74123

Special educational needs in the ordinary school.

Background: The project sought to investigate the nature of the curriculum provided for pupils with special educational needs who were being educated in ordinary schools. The particular focus was on pupils who were integrating into mainstream classes on an individual basis.
The research examined the modifications to curriculum, teaching strategies and resource materials used by teachers to manage pupils' learning in a mainstream setting.

Design: Three phases:
Initial interviews and data gathering;
In-depth studies;
Writing report and dissemination.

Size: Initial sample of 76 schools in 21 LEAs in England and Wales. In-depth study of 26 schools.

Methods: The initial phase of the project was spent in gathering information on pupils with special needs at present in ordinary schools. During the second phase of the research a number of schools were selected for intensive study. These covered the range of approaches or methods identified. In each the main effort was concentrated on how programmes of work were arrived at for the pupil or pupils in question and on how teachers implemented these in mainstream lessons. Schools in which staff were modifying or had recently modified the curriculum to take account of the needs of pupils with learning difficulties were included in order to document the process in detail. Research techniques utilized included interview, group discussion and classroom observation.

Results: The report focuses on academic organization, modifications to the curriculum, staffing and classroom teaching. Strategies that teachers found useful are pinpointed and areas where problems were encountered are discussed.

Date of Research: January 1982–December 1983.

Published Material: HEGARTY, S. (1985). 'Integration and teaching: some lessons from practice', *Educational Research*, **27**, 1.
CLUNIES-ROSS, L. (1984). 'Supporting the mainstream teacher', *Special Education: Forward Trends*, **11**, 3.
HODGSON, A. (1984). 'Integrating hearing impaired pupils', *Special Education: Forward Trends*, **11**, 4.
HODGSON, A. (1984). 'Integrating physically handicapped pupils', *Special Education: Forward Trends*, **11**, 1.
HODGSON, A., CLUNIES-ROSS, L., and HEGARTY, S. (1984). *Learning together: teaching pupils with special educational needs in the ordinary school.* Windsor: NFER-NELSON.

KEYWORDS: *curriculum development; integration; teaching approach; in-service education*

1/116   National Foundation for Educational   Moses, Diana, Ms
             Research   *Supervisor:* Hegarty, Seamus, Dr
             The Mere   (Special Needs)
             Upton Park
             Slough
             Berks. SL1 2DQ
             Tel: 0735-74123

Meeting special educational needs – support for the ordinary school.

Background: The study is concerned with how to provide practical support to schools in the task of meeting special educational needs. Its aims are:
(i) to examine the resources needed in different forms of special education provision in ordinary schools; (ii) to identify the criteria used for allocating resources in these situations; (iii) to examine different administrative structures within which resource needs can be determined and decisions on resource allocations taken.
Methods: The emphasis is on gathering and analysing qualitative data. Some questionnaire surveys are being conducted, but the main thrust of the work is to carry out detailed case studies.

Date of Research: October 1983–April 1986.

KEYWORDS: *integration; resource allocation; Education Act 1981; special school; INSET; support service*

National Hospitals College of Speech Sciences

1/117   NHCSS   Snowling, Margaret, Dr; Frith,
             59 Portland Street   Uta, Dr (Medical Research
             London W1   Council, Cognitive Development
             Tel: 01-636-1434   Unit)

An investigation of the reading performance of autistic children.

Background: The project originated from our previous work on developmental disorders of reading. Research on specific reading difficulties usually centres on individuals who have problems with word recognition and decoding skills. In contrast, autistic children are reported to decode well but to have comprehension difficulties. We aimed to explore their specific comprehension deficits.

Design: Autistic children have been compared with reading-age matched normal readers, dyslexic readers and mental-age matched ESN(M) children on a wide range of oral reading tasks.

Methods: Tests of single word reading; regular, irregular and nonwords lexical decision tasks.

Stroop tests

Cloze tests

Sentence: picture matching

Comprehension tests

Results: Autistic children can *decode* as well as R.A. matched normal and ESN readers and better than dyslexics. Autistic children exhibit normal phonological and syntactic processing but exhibit selective semantic deficits. Verbal ability predicts comprehension skill in autistic children, as it does in ESN(M) controls.

Date of Research: May 1981–Ongoing.

Published Material: FRITH, U. and SNOWLING, M. (1983). 'Reading for Sound and Reading for Meaning. A comparison of autistic, dyslexic and normal readers', *British Journal of Developmental Psychology*, **1**, 4, 329–342.

KEYWORDS: reading comprehension; autistic; dyslexia; ESN(M)

New College, Durham

1/118   Education Faculty   Brown, Ronald; Mason, Maggie,
           New College   Mrs
           Neville's Cross Centre   *Supervisors:* Brown, Ron;
           Nevilles Cross   Lawrenson, Wendy
           Durham DH1 4SY
           Tel: 0385-47325 ext. 278

The use of programmed learning approaches with children in Durham primary schools, with particular reference to language learning difficulties.

Background: There is a well-established link in theory between the need for individualization of learning for pupils experiencing language learning difficulties and the potential of programmed learning approaches to provide such individualization. Little work has been carried out in the field to establish whether such a connection is made in practice; therefore it is the intention of this study to survey the use of programmed learning approaches with pupils experiencing language learning difficulties to illuminate the area.

Design: In doing so it is hoped to uncover information on the attitudes of primary teachers to PL approaches and where appropriate examine such approaches that are employed in detail.

Size: 131 primary schools in County Durham were used with questionnaires being sent to 356 teachers.

Methods: Initial survey was by questionnaire which had been first piloted in eight schools. As a second stage 40 schools were selected for interviews with the headteachers and teachers responsible for special needs. Finally, four areas where the teachers claimed to have designed their own PL approach used participant observer methods to record the programmes in use.

Results: 1. Most PL approaches used in primary schools in the sample were commercial programmes – mainly SRA.
2. Teachers with a designated responsibility for special needs did tend to use PL approaches more.
3. Few teachers used self-designed programmes.
4. Those who had experience of PL approaches were more positive about them than those who didn't.

Date of Research: September 1981 – September 1983.

Published Material: Research Report (printed by Durham LEA and circulated to all junior schools): 'The use of Programmed Learning Approaches with Children in Durham Primary Schools, with Particular Reference to Language Learning Difficulties'.

KEYWORDS: language; learning difficulties; primary; programmed learning; individualized instruction

1/119   New College   Constable, Hilary, Dr; Brown,
             Neville's Cross Centre   Ron
             Neville's Cross
             Durham DH1 4SY
             Tel: 0385-47325

Facilitation of school-based curriculum development projects in schools meeting special needs of pupils.

Background: This study arises from views of school-based curriculum development, the teacher as researcher and action research, current in discussions about curriculum development. These ideas have placed the teacher at the centre of curriculum development, making demands for new skills, knowledge and attitudes. The study looks at one way in which College staff can facilitate this. It is hoped to draw some conclusions about in-service education from this.
Design: The study takes the form of case studies of consultancy activities by College staff in facilitating school based curriculum development' in meeting the special needs of pupils.
Size: So far two cases have been involved. The first comprised assisting a special school report its curriculum, and the second assisting the merger of a special and a mainstream school.
Methods: The methods used arise from participant observation, namely discussion, triangulation, action research.

Results: Results have been a greater awareness of the needs of staff and a more thoughtful approach to the activity. Tentative conclusions are that College staff were able to have a facilitating effect; an early demand for writing on the part of participants did ·much to focus on issues, and action was helped by focusing on controversial issues.

Date of Research: January 1982 – First school summer 1984; Second school summer 1986.

KEYWORDS: school-based innovation; consultancy; in-service education; curriculum development; teacher-based research

Newcastle upon Tyne Polytechnic

1/120   Newcastle upon Tyne Polytechnic   Whittaker, Christopher A.;
               Coach Lane Campus   Beavers, Hilary, Ms
               Newcastle-upon-Tyne NE7 7XA
               Tel: 0632-326002

A longitudinal study of aspects of the play of a Down's syndrome and a non-handicapped child during the first two years of life.

Background: The aim of the study is twofold – to obtain edited videotape to use in distance learning packages, seminars etc., in initial and in-service special education work, and to obtain naturalistic longitudinal data on the interrelationships between aspects of play, disability and prelinguistic communication in the first two years.
Size: The children are first-born infants of professional parents – a Down's boy and a non-handicapped girl.
Methods: Videotape at five to six week intervals in the children's own home. Data is collected on solitary play, mother–child interaction and researcher–child interaction, although these transitions are not rigidly prescribed. The children are encouraged to play with their own toys with the occasional introduction of novel equipment. The emphasis during data collection is on informality, in order to attempt to obtain naturalistic behaviour from the participants.

Results: Data in preliminary stage of analysis.

Date of Research: November 1982–Easter 1985.

KEYWORDS: prelinguistic communication; play; Down's syndrome; videotape; teacher education; pre-school

North East London Polytechnic

1/121   School of Education and Humanities   Green, Len; Francis, Jean, Mrs
               North East London Polytechnic
               Longbridge Road
               Dagenham
               Essex RM8 2AS
               Tel: 01-590-7722

Children's learning skills and school attainment.

Background: Reliability and validity studies of Stott's Guide to the Child's Learning Skills.
Design: Relationship between children's learning skills (behaviours) and their later attainments in reading, number and spoken language.
Size: 2272 five and six year old children in infants' schools. Follow up 1157 of same sample at age nine and ten (intended further follow-up in secondary stage).
Methods: Teacher completion of The Guide to the Child's Learning Skills (GCLS); teacher assessment of attainments; case studies of discordant children (sub-sample check with standardized tests).

Results: Illustration of strong links between the way children behave in learning situations and their later attainments. Evidence for the reliability and validity of GCLS. Contribution of this approach for increasing teacher awareness of individual needs.

Date of Research: September 1977–Final completion expected 1985.

Published Material: FRANCIS, J. and GREEN. L. (1984). 'Investigating Children's Learning Skills in the Classroom'. In: *New Frontiers*, Report of the National Conference of the National Council for Special Education. Stratford-upon-Avon: N.C.S.E.
GREEN, L. and FRANCIS, J. 'Helping Young Children with Special Educational Needs', *Remedial Education*, **15**, 1, Feb. 1980, 17–22.
GREEN, L., FRANCIS, J. and STOTT. D. (1984). 'Confirmation of the Relationship between Children's Learning Styles and Attainments by Examination of Discordant Cases', *Human Learning*, **3**, 4, Dec.
STOTT, D.H. (1978). *Helping Children with Learning Difficulties: a Diagnostic Teaching Approach.* London: Ward Lock.
STOTT, D.H., GREEN, L. and FRANCIS, J. (1983). *Guide to the Child's Learning Skills.* Stafford: National Association for Remedial Education.
STOTT, D.H., GREEN, L. and FRANCIS, J. (1983). 'Learning Style and School Attainment', *Human Learning*, **2**, 1, 61–74.

KEYWORDS: learning skills; screening; attainment; Stott's guide; primary

1/122   School of Education and Humanities   Vincent, Denis
               North East London Polytechnic
               Longbridge Road
               Dagenham
               Essex RM8 2AS
               Tel: 01-590-7722

The diagnostic spelling test – longitudinal study.

Background: (1) To compare longitudinal performance on a diagnostic spelling test of normal and backward spellers. (2) To relate backwardness in spelling to learning difficulties in general, and reading in particular.

Design: Longitudinal study of three 'cohorts' of 2nd and 3rd year pupils tested at six month intervals between September 1982 and 1983. Additional data, including Stott's Guide to Children's Learning Difficulties, obtained for backward spellers.

Size: Initial sample 1604 children, complete data for 1427, 270 backward spellers included.

Methods: Random samples of schools in England and Wales who had participated in standardization of NFER-NELSON Diagnostic Spelling Test were asked to participate in a longitudinal follow-up of progress in spelling throughout a school year, using the DST. The opportunity was taken to obtain additional data about children with low initial scores – this included Stott's Guide and a teacher questionnaire.

Results: Main analysis of results has concentrated on progress statistics for whole sample, but further detailed analysis will be made of data for backward spellers. This will include incidence of general learning difficulties and extent to which spelling difficulty is associated with reading difficulty.

Date of Research: April 1982–Due Autumn 1984.

Published Material: VINCENT, D. and CLAYDON, J. (1982). *Diagnostic Spelling Test.* Windsor: NFER NELSON.

KEYWORDS: spelling; backward speller; Stott's guide; reading; diagnostic spelling test; longitudinal

North East Wales Institute of Higher Education

1/123   The North East Wales Institute   Jones, E.V.
             Cefn Road
             Wrexham
             Clwyd LL13 9NE
             Tel: 0978-359221

The integration of spina bifida children into ordinary schools.
Design: Comparison of Clwyd and Mid Glamorgan's integration efforts – through case histories.
Size: To be decided.
Methods: Case histories.

Date of Research: October 1984 – 1987

KEYWORDS: integration; spina bifida

North London Polytechnic

1/124   Social Studies Department   Lumley, Anthony
             Polytechnic of North London
             Holloway Road
             London N7 8DB
             Tel: 01-607-2789

Development of recreation techniques with low-functioning visually hearing impaired young people.

Background: To bring together teams of people to develop techniques in recreation and communication with the client group.
Design: To test ideas over short periods possibly once or twice a year over three years.
Size: Ten communicators and ten young people aged 16 – 23 years in each of two series.
Methods: Using recreational equipment such as cloths, hoops, rings, balloons, vinyl balls, plastic sticks, rhythm and music. Supplemented with special toys and computer programs.

Results: Reports available June 1984.

Date of Research: 1982 – 1985.

Published Material: Individual reports availability refer to Anthony Lumley, Mobility International, 62 Union Street, London SE1 1TD.

KEYWORDS: deaf/blind; recreation; play; adult

North Nottinghamshire College of Further Education

1/125	Work Orientation Unit North Nottinghamshire College of Further Education Carlton Road Worksop Notts. Tel: 0909-473561	Smith, Perry; Braund, Michael *Supervisor:* Hutchinson, D.

Computer Programs for the student with moderate learning difficulties in FE.

Background: The aims of the programs are as an aid to the teaching of Social Education.
Design: The project will develop and test eight programs as described.
Size: Testing to be undertaken locally and in college.
Methods: Testing carried out by local teachers and FE staff.

Results: A suite of programs will be developed and returned to the MEP for publishing.

Date of Research: February 1984–January 1985.

KEYWORDS: microcomputer; software; moderate learning difficulties; further education; social education

1/126	Work Orientation Unit North Nottinghamshire College of Further Education Carlton Road Worksop Notts. Tel: 0909-473561	Tennyson, Carol, Mrs *Supervisor:* Hutchinson, D.

Transition to adulthood for severely physically handicapped students

Background: The aim of the project is to develop a college-based curriculum which will help severely physically handicapped students for whom the prospect of employment is unlikely to make the transition from school to adult life.
Design: The curriculum has been designed around five broad-based subject areas: personal care; mobility; general education; social education and recreation. Throughout the course the emphasis is on life after college, and students are actively encouraged to take steps towards establishing life-styles which they will find enjoyable and rewarding.
Methods: Curriculum design; implementation; evaluation.

Date of Research: January 1985–December 1985.

KEYWORDS: transition to adult life; physical handicap; curriculum development; further education.

1/127	Child Development Research Unit Nottingham University University Park Nottingham NG7 2RD Tel: 0602-56101	Miller, Andrew

Parental participation in paired reading: a controlled study and an examination of the role of the technique in home–school collaboration.

Design: A double-blind controlled study of the effects of paired reading was carried out with 33 failing readers and their parents.
Size: The children were aged 8 to 11 and had reading delays of at least 18 months.

Results: After a mean time of 7.6 hours of paired reading at home, spread over 6 weeks, the children made gains of 2.43 months for reading accuracy and 4.36 months for reading comprehension, compared with a control group which experienced respective gains of 0.81 months and 1.69 months. The differences were statistically significant for accuracy but not for comprehension. The usefulness of the paired reading technique as a stimulus to home–school collaboration schemes is also discussed.

Date of Research: January 1981–July 1984.

Published Material: BUSHELL, R., MILLER, A., and ROBSON, D. (1982). 'Parents as remedial teachers: an account of a paired reading project with junior school failing readers and their parents', *AEP Journal*, **5,** 9, 7–13.
ROBSON, D., MILLER, A., and BUSHELL, R. (1984). 'The development of paired reading in High Peak and West Derbyshire', *Remedial Education*, **19,** 4 November.

KEYWORDS: parents; paired reading; reading difficulties; primary

1/128   School of Education   Jones, Philip Richard
             University of Nottingham   *Supervisor:* Stratford, Brian, Dr
             University Park
             Nottingham NG7 2RD
             Tel: 0602-56101

The pictorial embellishment of the basic text to establish a visual vocabulary in pre-school children and the mentally disabled.

Background: Until relatively recently most mentally handicapped people were not considered capable of learning an orthodox print vocabulary. This investigation considered the effectiveness of representational accentuation (i.e. changing the shape of print) and the pictorial elaboration of print in comparison with more conventional cueing in establishing other styles of vocabulary (e.g. Blissymbols).
Design: A series of experimental studies looking at the effectiveness of a variety of representational cues. Time series assessment was utilized. The design straddles the refined control of laboratory and action research programmes to try to maximize practical relevance.
Size: ESN(S) and other developmentally young (nursery) children studied as small group and single subject, sampled on a described but opportunity basis.
Methods: Subjects were always self-matched within studies and conditions were comparable so that some inter-experimental inferences could be made. Flash cards were used with the cue on one side and the print or symbol on the other.

Results: Preliminary results indicate the general superiority of elaborated or accentuated forms in comparison with picture-cued or just verbal-cued learning.

Date of Research: Main study: September 1983–August 1987.

Published Material: JONES, P.R. (1983). 'Symbol Accentuation: A Controlled Comparison Of Its Effectiveness For Teaching Initial Word Recognition to Mentally Handicapped Pupils, Division of Educational and Child Psychology - B.P.S. Papers 1983. **7** 1, 24–30.

KEYWORDS: *mental handicap; reading; symbol accentuation; graphic symbol; blissymbols; pre-school; ESN(S)*

1/129   School of Education   Palmer, E.A., Miss
            University of Nottingham   *Supervisor:* Stratford, B., Dr
            University Park
            Nottingham NG7 2RD
            Tel: 0602-56101

Perception of depth in Down's syndrome children

Background: As a follow up to the Author's MEd dissertation (available at the Main Library, University of Nottingham) on visual perception in Down's children, this study investigates depth perception – comparing it to groups of normal infants and other mentally subnormal children, matched on mental age. The main aim is to investigate whether the behaviour on a series of visual depth perception tasks by the Down's syndrome group is completely idiosyncratic, or whether it is comparable to one or both of the other two experimental groups.

Size: Subjects are constantly being accumulated. For each *individual* experiment, three groups of between 8 and 20 are used. The *total* number of subjects in the whole series of experiments will be upwards of 150.

Methods: A series of experiments involving block designs and models where the phenomena of height in plane, graduated texture, and receding size are utilized to investigate the capacity of the three groups to (a) recognize, and (b) reproduce the phenomenon of visual depth.

Results: At present, tentative results suggests that the behaviour of the Down's syndrome group is comparable to that of young normal infants. At any rate their behaviour is more unified (as a group) than that of the undifferentiated mentally subnormal group. There is also some evidence for certain idiosyncratic behaviour.

Date of Research: April 1981 – (not before) July 1985.

KEYWORDS: *Down's syndrome; depth perception; severe learning difficulties*

Open University

1/130   Department of the Psychology of   Corbett, Jenny, Ms
            Education   *Supervisor:* Booth, Tony
            The Open University
            Walton Hall
            Milton Keynes MK7 6AA
            Tel: 0908-74066

Integration in further education: a case study.

Background: The background is an integration scheme, which has been established since 1981, at Tottenham Technical College. The aims are to illustrate the practice of integration.

Design: The investigation is designed in four sections: (1) a national perspective on integration in further education; (2) the policies and practice of integration in one borough; (3) integration in one college 1981–4; (4) conclusion. The scope is to offer a

national perspective, and then to focus upon the practice in one college over three years.
Size: The size of the sample of handicapped students is about 50, varying over a three year period. All except two are physically handicapped.
Methods: Detailed recording of day-to-day progress has been used, as well as recording of reactions of staff and students. The records have been collected through two distinct phases:
1981–2: A pilot scheme.
1982–4: Development of a course and access for students.
The changes which these developments brought about have been recorded in detail.

Results: The results compare with the findings of Hegarty and Pocklington, as regards mistakes made in the pilot scheme, and initial problems of adjustment. The development of a special course, which sets FE apart from the comprehensive school pattern, has created a broader clientele and more open access into further education.

Date of Research: 1980–End of 1985.

KEYWORDS: integration; further education; physical handicap; curriculum development; educational provision

1/131   Institute of Educational Technology   Hawkridge, David G., Prof.;
             The Open University   Vincent, Tom, Dr; Hales, Gerald,
             Walton Hall   Dr
             Milton Keynes MK7 6AA
             Tel: 0908-653216

New information technology and the education of disabled children and adults.

Background: This study was carried out specifically to serve as the foundation for a state-of-the-art book.
Design: It encompassed schools, universities, hospitals, research laboratories and commercial companies in the United Kingdom and the United States; in fact, it included any institution or individual trying to do R & D on information technology applications in the education of physically handicapped, blind, deaf or speech-impaired children or adults. Data were collected by the three principal researchers, plus two consultants (one in each country), by letter, telephone, interviews and visiting.

Results: Results and conclusions are being published in book form and are too extensive to summarize. The book deals particularly with experience in using the technology and problems encountered.

Date of Research: February 1983–April 1984.

Published Material: HAWKRIDGE, D.G., VINCENT, T. & HALES, G. (1984). *New information technology in the education of disabled children and adults.* Beckenham, Kent: Croom Helm.

KEYWORDS: physical handicap; hearing impairment; visual impairment; information technology

1/132   Institute of Educational Technology   Vincent, Thomas, Dr
             The Open University
             Walton Hall
             Milton Keynes MK7 6AA
             Tel: 0908-653781

Information technology for disabled undergraduates in distance education.

Background: To assess new developments in information technology in relation to the needs of disabled undergraduate students in distance education. Specific needs that have been identified:
1) Blind students – preparation of course work for a sighted tutor when student's working medium is Braille.
2) Deaf students – communication with a tutor by telephone.
3) Physically handicapped students – preparation of course work and examinations with limited manual motor control.
Design: Methods have been designed to enable disabled students to use information technology hardware to meet the needs outlined above. In some cases, software development has been necessary to change the function of the hardware.
Size: Twelve disabled students involved in development work.
Methods: Information technology assessed:
1) Blind students: (a) microcomputer/synthetic speech (Braille input (Perkins)); (b) Brailink terminal from home via telephone.
2) Deaf students; (a) visual display telephone (Vistel); (b) Viewdata/electronic mail for communication.
3) Physically handicapped students: microwriter for written communication (essays, letters, exams).

Results: There is little doubt of the value of information technology for disabled people in distance education – overcoming communication problems has been an important aspect of the development.

Date of Research: December 1979–Ongoing.

Published Material: 'CAL for blind students: some recent developments', *Aids, communication and electronics*, **2**, 1982.
'Distance teaching and the visually handicapped', *ICDE bulletin*, **1**, 1983.
'Home-based computing facilities for visually handicapped students', *Teaching at a Distance*, 23, 1983.
'Microcomputers and synthetic speech: some experiences', *The New Beacon: The Journal of Blind Welfare*, Sept. 1983, **57**, 797, pp. 225–227.
'A microcomputer Linked Voice Synthesizer', *Computers & Education*, **6**, 1, 1982.

KEYWORDS: *distance education; information technology; microcomputer; physical handicap; hearing impairment; visual impairment*

1/133   Institute of Educational Technology   Vincent, Thomas, Dr
            The Open University
            Walton Hall
            Milton Keynes MK7 6AA
            Tel: 0908-653781

Microcomputers and synthetic speech for visually handicapped children.

Background: To develop synthetic speech as an output medium for a computer to enable visually handicapped children to use a computer.
Application areas: learning Braille; programming; Braille transcription.
Design: The investigation involved the development of software for microcomputer (synthetic speech output) for the above applications.
Size: 15 schools equipped with a microcomputer workstation (disk drive, printer, speech synthesizer, Perkins Braille, concept keyboard) for evaluation/development of software.
Methods: Software developed to meet needs defined by teachers from the schools involved in the collaborative development.

Results: Eight computer programs making up a package suitable for schools for the visually handicapped are a direct outcome of the research. The other important outcome is the knowledge of techniques that enable a blind pupil to effectively use a microcomputer with speech output.

Date of Research: March 1982–December 1984.

Published Material: 'A talking Brailler', *Insight*, **4**, 2, 1982.
'Talking Basic and Talking Braille: two applications of synthetic speech', *Computer Education*, 45, 1983.

KEYWORDS: synthetic speech; visual impairment; Braille; software; microcomputer

Oxford Polytechnic

1/134   Department of Educational   Thomas, Gareth
              Development
              Oxford Polytechnic
              Lady Spencer Churchill College
              Wheatley
              Oxon OX9 1HX

Room management in mainstream education.

Background: Integration of special needs children brings problems in terms of investing time to those children and to the rest of the class. With increased parental involvement in schools and involvement of support services in the classroom, the aim was to determine whether room management, a system of classroom organization, could maximize the potential of such personnel, in meeting the needs of all the children in a classroom.
Design: Repeated measures design of one classroom under three conditions:
(a) Classroom functioning only with teacher;
(b) Classroom functioning with teacher and parents;
(c) Classroom functioning as in (b) above but using room management.
Size: 4th year junior class. 21 children observed.
Methods: Videotape analysis of children's engagement under the three conditions. On-task/off-task dichotomy used.

Results: Analysis of variance and post hoc tests showed significant differences existing between all conditions, with engagement under (c) highest.
It was tentatively concluded that room management may usefully structure the activity of personnel in the classroom.

Date of Research: March 1984–September 1984.

KEYWORDS: classroom organization; integration; room management; primary

Oxford University

1/135   Department of Educational Studies   Postlethwaite, Keith; Hackney,
              University of Oxford   Ann, Dr; Raban, Bridie, Ms
              15 Norham Gardens
              Oxford OX2 6PY
              Tel: 0865-54121

Programme of research on children with special educational needs.

Background: The research programme is concerned with two main themes:
(a) The training of mainstream teachers in relation to special educational needs.
(b) School-based provision for children with special educational needs.
In connection with these two themes, the aims are to provide a survey of current practice and to study some examples of this practice in detail.
Design: Thus a preliminary survey of special needs aspects of teacher training in university departments in England and Wales has been followed by case study in nine of these universities; and a preliminary survey of special and comprehensive schools in Oxfordshire has been followed by case studies in four schools. In relation to the teacher training theme, an evaluation of the impact of an Oxfordshire initiative in in-service training has also been completed.
The programme also encompasses two specific studies on:
 (i) the management of disruptive pupils;
(ii) the educational experiences of children who were medically 'at risk' at birth.
Methods: The main methods in use are: structured interviews; questionnaires; classroom observation; social skills training; infant screening schedules; survey of school documents including pupil records.

Date of Research: September 1982–August 1986.

Published Material: LABON, D. (1984). 'Special Education Aspects of University P.G.C.E. Courses', *J. Further & Higher Educ.*, **8,** 1, Spring.

KEYWORDS: *teacher training; in-service education; integration; behaviour problem.*

Portsmouth Polytechnic

1/136   Department of Psychology   Buckley, S.J., Mrs
               Portsmouth Polytechnic
               King Charles Street
               Portsmouth PO1 2ER
               Tel: 0705-827681

The effect of early educational programmes on the development of the Down's syndrome child and on their families.

Background: To evaluate the effect of intensive home teaching on the rate of development of Down's syndrome children and factors which might affect their rate of progress.
To investigate the effects of such a teaching programme on the families.
Size: Sample of 14 pre-school Down's syndrome children – all those in 2–4 year age group in two health districts.
Methods: Each family received regular home-teaching over $2\frac{1}{2}$–3 year period half weekly visits, the other half fortnightly visits. Continuous records of the child's progress on Portage were kept and Griffiths' DQs at the outset and annually thereafter.

Results: Interim results for first two years – summary. Wide individual differences were found in the progress of the children. All benefited to some degree from the teaching but with wide variation. The data suggests that the rate of progress declined during periods of family stress. The children in families with a young baby born during the period of study showed the least progress. The weekly visits were possibly more effective than fortnightly. Some parents found the teaching role an additional source of anxiety.

Date of Research: October 1980–1984.

Published Material: BUCKLEY, S.J. (1984). 'The effect of early home teaching on the development of children with Down's Syndrome and their families'. (Paper presented to British Psychological Society Conference 1984 Warwick University). In: Daley, B. (Ed) (1985) *Portage: The Importance of Parents* (Proceedings of 3rd Portage Conference). Windsor: NFER-NELSON.
BUCKLEY, S.J. (1984). 'The influence of family variables on Portage'. In: Dessent, A. (Ed) *What is important about Portage?* Windsor: NFER-NELSON.

KEYWORDS: *early education; portage; Down's syndrome; pre-school; home teaching; family*

1/137	School of Educational Studies	Eskdale, Ronald
	Portsmouth Polytechnic	
	Locksway Road	
	Portsmouth PO4 8JF	
	Tel: 0705-735241 ext. 264	

Organization and provision for children with special educational needs in middle schools.

Background: The aim of the study is to investigate the various ways in which two 8–12 urban middle schools make provision for children with special educational needs.
Design: Particular attention is focused on the following: (1) the different perspectives on special educational needs; (2) transfer procedures; (3) decision making; (4) links with agencies outside the school.
Size: Two urban middle schools.
Methods: Observation; interviews; questionnaires.

Date of Research: December 1980–December 1985.

KEYWORDS: *management; middle school; whole school; programme evaluation*

1/138	School of Educational Studies	May, Denis, Dr
	Portsmouth Polytechnic	
	Locksway Road	
	Portsmouth PO4 8JF	
	Tel: 0705-735241 ext. 250	

Alternative environments for special education: a self evaluative case study of open air camp schools.

Background: To explore the possibility of integrating children of varying backgrounds in a self-contained community to provide extra dimensions for understanding the individual problems associated with primary labelling.
Design: To set up teaching projects based on a craft theme, i.e. building, craftwork (wood, clay, wool, etc.). The subsidiary theme is language competence and notions concerning socialization.
Size: Eight school camps × 45 children.
Methods: Teaching projects; community discussion; one-to-one relationships; ethnographic analysis of above.

Results: Paper in process of writing.

Date of Research: 1977–1984/5.

Published Material: PARKER, S. (1983). 'If you go down to the woods today', *TES*, 9.8.83.

KEYWORDS camp school; crafts

Radlett School for Autistic Children

1/139   Radlett School for Autistic Children   Jordan, Rita, Mrs
           Harper Lane
           Radlett
           Herts.
           Tel: 09276-4922

An evaluation of the use of microcomputers in the education of autistic children.

Background: An initial feasibility study, commissioned by the National Autistic Society, investigated the role of computer-assisted learning in the education of autistic children. This recommended a range of equipment and suggested an evaluation study be conducted on the usefulness of this equipment, and available software, in meeting those particular educational needs.

Design: The study will last for four months only and so will not be able to show long-term benefits or disadvantages. It will look in a general way at staff use of and attitudes to the new technology and how it is incorporated into the curriculum of the school. It will take note of any particular reactions of the children in the light of their previous behaviour, and use the experience of the staff in teaching autistic children to evaluate the usefulness of what is offered, and ways it might be improved.

Size: There are 33 autistic children in the school and a staff of 16, including seven qualified teachers.

Methods: A questionnaire to all staff pre and post the study will examine any changes in staff attitudes. A record of use of all equipment and programs with all the children will show how attitudes affect use and how the curriculum has adapted to meet the new technology. Records of all the sessions (plus some video recording) will show any particular reactions of the children, and teachers' recorded comments and suggestions will be assessed. In addition, the study will look for any generalization of computer-learnt skills into other situations.

Date of Research: March 1984–September 1984.

KEYWORDS: computer assisted learning; autistic; microcomputer; software

Ravenswood Village

1/140   Ravenswood Village   Iggulden, Leonard C.
           Ninemile Ride
           Crowthorne
           Berks.

Microcomputer applications in special education.

Background: To introduce staff and residents to the potential of microcomputers in the education of severely handicapped persons.

Design: 1) Collect, and where possible, adapt existing software; 2) Develop new software to meet needs; 3) Develop computer controlled interactive environment.

Date of Research: September 1983–November 1984.

KEYWORDS: software; microcomputer

Reading University

1/141   Department of Linguistic Science   Crystal, David, Prof.
               University of Reading
               Whiteknights
               Reading RG6 2AA
               Tel: 0734-875123 ext. 380

The diagnosis of language disorders in children.

Background: To identify linguistically defined syndromes in children, using the techniques of clinical linguistics.
Design: Linguistic profiles are made of spontaneous speech samples of the children, based on their phonological, grammatical and semantic features. Each sample is analysed statistically, and clusters of diagnostic features are identified. A comparative analysis leads to the establishment of group profiles on the basis of which a set of linguistic syndromes will be postulated.
Methods: Each child is studied on the basis of two 50-turn samples, extracted from 30/45 minute clinical sessions at University clinic. See Crystal, D., *Profiling Linguistic Disability*, Arnold 1982.

Date of Research: January 1984–July 1985.

KEYWORDS: language disorder; linguistic profile; phonology.

Rehabilitation Engineering Unit

1/142   Rehabilitation Engineering Unit   Thornett, Carole, Dr
               Chailey Heritage (School Hospital)   *Supervisor:* Brown, A.W.S.
               North Chailey
               Lewes BN8 4EF
               Sussex

Microcomputer interfacing – the development of a universal patient-operated switch assessment and prescription device.

Background: This proposal is concerned with the development of a patient-operated switch assessment and prescription unit which will result in the most appropriate controls being provided for severely physically handicapped children, predominantly those with cerebral palsy, who need to use electronic communication aids, microcomputers or other assistive equipment. It is hoped that the research will yield equipment and techniques which will have a wide application in special schools and in establishments such as the Communication Aids Centres recently set up by the DHSS.

Design: Recent advances in microelectronic and microcomputer technology have allowed the development of extremely sophisticated aids for disabled people, and have led to the acceptance of computers as a commonplace and often indispensable part of school and everyday life. Suitable research into the ways in which such equipment can be used by physically disabled people has been largely neglected, however, and many potential users are denied the advantages of this technology because of the inadequate provision of an 'interface' between the user and the equipment.

The equipment produced will allow assessment of a child's ability to learn to use switches or other transducers in a motivational environment by controlling electronic toys, music or video games.

Date of Research: April 1984 – June 1986.

KEYWORDS: *microcomputer; communication; assessment; cerebral palsy; physical handicap.*

Royal Association for Disability and Rehabilitation

1/143   The Royal Association for Disability   Bookis, Joan, Miss (Enquiries to
           and Rehabilitation   Mrs Judith Male, Education
           25 Mortimer Street   Officer, RADAR)
           London W1N 8AB   *Supervisors:* Massie, Bert
           Tel: 01-637-5400   (Executive Assistant to the
                                                      Director, RADAR); Kettle,
                                                      Melvyn, Dr (Applied Psychology
                                                      Dept., University of Aston)

Beyond the school gate: a study of disabled young people aged 13–19.

Background: Concern about the future of disabled school leavers, in particular those with physical disabilities including those with multiple disabilities.
Aims: 1. to establish the numbers of disabled youngsters leaving school; 2. to determine their disabilities; 3. to determine additional problems they face (above those faced by all youngsters); 4. to consider the concept of 'significant living without work'.
Design: National postal survey of schools (both special and ordinary) which were known to have children with physical disabilities, and interviews with disabled young people in four areas – London, Merseyside, W. Midlands and Wiltshire/Gloucester.
Size: Questionnaires returned on 1289 pupils; interviews with 864 pupils; interviews with 19 Specialist Careers Officers.
Methods: Postal survey and individual interviews.

Results: Bleak future facing disabled young people. Need for more independence and self-care training in schools. More social integration needed. More contact needed between schools and employers. Disabled youngsters expect to find work eventually. Specialist Careers Service under considerable strain and not able to meet the needs of disabled youngsters as well as many officers would wish.

Date of Research: October 1981 – October 1983.

Published Material: BOOKIS, J. (1983). *Beyond the School Gate.* London: RADAR, October.

KEYWORDS: physical handicap; school leaver

Royal National Institute for the Deaf

1/144   Scientific and Technical Department   Wright, Richard
Royal National Institute for the Deaf
105 Gower Street
London WC1E 6AH
Tel: 01-387-8033

The development of a microcomputer-based visual speech display.

Background: The aim of the research has been to develop a display of speech pitch and energy, a spectrum display, and a hearing aid tester, all based on a generally available microcomputer. The research includes the development of structured speech-work schemes for use with the display.

Date of Research: Ongoing.

Published Material: KING, A., PARKER, A., SPANNER, M., and WRIGHT, R. (1982). 'A Speech Display Computer for use in Schools for the Deaf' in Proceedings of the IEEE International Conference on Acoustics, Speech and Signal Processing, 1982, **2,** 755–758.

KEYWORDS: speech display; microcomputer; visual feedback; hearing impairment

St. Andrew's College of Education, Glasgow

1/145   St. Andrew's College of Education   McGregor, June, Mrs (Music);
Courthill   Rankin, Irene, Mrs (Speech &
Bearsden   Drama)
Glasgow
Tel: 041-943-1424

An examination of the influence of school-based in-service work on the wider curriculum through the use of music and speech and drama with non-specialists in these areas.

Background: The research has arisen out of the school-based in-service work carried out at the instigation of the Adviser in Special Education (Renfrew division). The aim is to discover whether this approach can leave non-specialist staff capable and confident of intregrating and developing the subjects within the curriculum.
Design: Weekly morning sessions of a practical nature, followed by discussion and evaluation in the afternoon and supported by audio and visual material designed especially for the groups concerned.
Size: The whole school, with a roll of 46 children with severe learning difficulties, will become involved, although at present two classes are being concentrated upon.
Methods: Demonstration; Team-teaching; Self-evaluation along with discussion; Class assessment through use of video.

Date of Research: October 1983–Ongoing.

KEYWORDS: in-service education; non-specialist staff; curriculum development; music; speech and drama; severe learning difficulties

1/146   St. Andrew's College of Education   Tollan, John, H., Dr; Dixon, John,
          Department of Special Education   K.
          Needs
          Bearsden
          Glasgow
          Tel: 041-943-1424

'Micros in Special Education' – An evaluation of an innovatory strategy for the introduction of microcomputers into ESN(M) schools in Strathclyde.

Background: Following a survey of MMH schools which established the high levels of teacher anxiety and apprehension concerning the imminent introduction of microcomputers, a St. Andrew's College/Strathclyde Region working party was set up with the aim of identifying an effective strategy for their innovation. The strategy adopted was designed to give the teachers the confidence to use available school hardware and develop relevant software, and thus set the innovation of micros within the context of a 'whole school' policy on the use of micros as a means of enhancing their school curricula.

Design: In-service staff development booklets and accompanying software produced by the Working party and piloted in 4 MMH schools are now being disseminated into the MMH schools in the six divisions in Strathclyde Region (Ayrshire, Argyle, Dunbarton, Glasgow, Lanarkshire, Renfrewshire).

Size: Pilot Study: 4 MMH schools (1 primary, 1 secondary, 2 all-through schools). 38 teachers.

Full Study: 41 MMH schools. 400 teachers.

Methods:

1. *Production of three in-service staff development booklets*
(i) Managing the Micro – familiarization of staff with hardware. (ii) Tackling the Task – introduction of staff to writing algorithms. (iii) Enhancing the Curriculum – 'whole school' curriculum planning using the microcomputers as a means of enhancing methodology and content.

2. *Setting up of a regional resource centre*
(i) Software library of programs specified by teachers and written by project programmers. (ii) Evaluation of collated commercial software to provide guidelines for schools on appropriateness. (iii) Hardware display area for schools to examine current developments.

3. *Provision of programming support service*
(i) A full-time programmer for each division to service the algorithms produced by school working groups.

4. *Dissemination strategy*
(i) A coordinator and two staff tutors for each division are responsible for staff development and support. (ii) A school coordinator from each school is responsible for introducing and evaluating project materials in their school. (iii) The project supervisor (MSC-funded) coordinates the link between divisional coordinators and programmers and the facilities of the resource centre (including access to a view data terminal). (iv) The project assistant (MSC-funded) develops and operates the software library and provides monthly updates on available project and commercial software evaluations.

5. *Evaluation Strategy*

Date of Research: April 1982–April 1986.

Published Material: Booklets: (1) TOLLAN, J.H. *et al* (1983). *Managing the Micro.* (2) TOLLAN, J.H. *et al.* (1983). *Tackling the Task.* (3) TOLLAN, J.H. *et al.* (1984). *Enhancing the Curriculum.* (All published by St. Andrew's College, Glasgow.)
Articles: (1) DIXON, J.K. *et al.* (1984). *The St. Andrew's College Project.* Published in the Micro Primer (special) Pack, Scottish Microelectronics Development Programme.

KEYWORDS: microcomputer; ESN(M) schools; curriculum development; resource centre; whole school; software; in-service education

Scottish Council for Research in Education

1/147   Scottish Council for Research in   Corrie, Malcolm
           Education
           15 St. John Street
           Edinburgh EH8 8JR

Further education for the handicapped.

Background: To offer an illuminative account of four separate studies of ongoing developments, indicating problems and constraints.
Study 1 – leavers' programmes.
Study 2 – FE provision for handicapped students.
Study 3 – educational efforts of Training Centres.
Study 4 – longitudinal study of transition of a group of handicapped pupils from school to FE and employment.
Design: Case study, illuminative approach.

Results: Extension to project has delayed results.

Date of Research: September 1980 – December 1983.

Published Material: CORRIE, M. and ZAKLUKIEWICZ, S. (1982). Leavers' programmes in special education. Paper given at the Lothian Region/Murray House Joint In-service course for staff in special schools.
CORRIE, M. (1982). On from special school. Paper given at the Jordanhill College in-service course for specialist staff in special schools, further education colleges, adult training centres and careers services.
CORRIE, M. (1983). *Leaving special school: report on the first stage of a study of special school leavers.* Edinburgh: Scottish Council for Research in Education (Project Working Paper 1).
ZAKLUKIEWICZ, S. (1984). *Developments in day care: case studies of day care provision for mentally handicapped adults and young people.* Edinburgh: Scottish Council for Research in Education. (Project Working Paper 2).
CORRIE, M. (1984). *After special school: a study of leavers from special schools.* Edinburgh: Scottish Council for Research in Education. (Project Working Paper 3).
ZAKLUKIEWICZ, S. and CORRIE, M. (1984). *Further education and special needs: case studies of provision.* Edinburgh: Scottish Council for Research in Education. (Project Working Paper 4).
ZAKLUKIEWICZ, S. (1984). *Southbrae: a case study of development in day services for mentally handicapped adults.* Edinburgh: Scottish Council for Research in Education (Project Working Paper 5).
CORRIE, M. and ZAKLUIEWICZ, S. (1984). Qualitative research and case study approaches: an introduction. Paper given at the Economic and Social Research Council conference on research methods in special education at London University.

KEYWORDS: post-16; further education; leavers' programmes; vocational education; transition to adult life; longitudinal

1/148   Scottish Council for Research in   Corrie, Malcolm
           Education
           15 St John Street
           Edinburgh EH8 8JR

Educational opportunities for young people with special educational needs.

Background: The chief aim is to report on policy and provision relating to the range of opportunities for education and training for young poeple in the 16–18 age group with special educational needs, and to discuss the issues and implications for further practical development. The report is intended to serve as an informative and comprehensive document for education authorities with responsibilities and interests in relation to provision for young people with special needs.

Design: The project is focused on policy and provision in the following sectors:
– further education provision, including mainstream courses, link and bridging courses, special courses and units, outreach schemes;
– educational provision in adult training centres, day centres, and sheltered workshops;
– vocational training and education schemes provided through the MSC;
– school-based provision through staying on/transfer and school/FE links.

Methods: Written enquiries, documentary material, interviews, and questionnaires where appropriate.

Date of Research: January 1984–February 1986.

Published Material: CORRIE, M. and ZAKLUKIEWICZ, S. (1984). 'Leaving Special Education: Issues for Research', *Scottish Educational Review*, **16,** 1.
CORRIE, M. and ZAKLUKIEWICZ, S. (1984). *Qualitative Research in Special Education: Case Study Approaches.* ESRC Workshop on Evaluation Methodology in Special Education.
CORRIE, M. (1983). *Leaving Special School.* Project working paper.
ZAKLUKIEWICZ, S. (1984). *Developments in Day Care.* Project working paper.

KEYWORDS: provision; post-16; training; further education; adult training centre

Scottish Micro-electronics Development Project

1/149   SMDP   Nash, V., Dr; Blythman, Marion
             74 Victoria Crescent Road
             Glasgow

The use of microcomputers with pupils with moderate learning difficulties.

Background: To provide approximately 25 programs to be used with the DTI issue of microcomputers to special schools and units in the UK.

Design: The project has been designed to involve classroom teachers, advisers and college of education staff in the development of software.

Methods: The aims have been to produce software designed to augment teaching skills and to provide computer-assisted learning across the various aspects of the curriculum for 14–16 year olds with moderate learning difficulties through involvement with teachers, etc.

Results: 25–30 programmes: still to be finally evaluated.

Date of Research: September 1983–September 1984 (end of project).

KEYWORDS: microcomputer; software; moderate learning difficulties; curriculum development; computer assisted learning

Sheffield City Polytechnic

1/150   Department of Education
Sheffield City Polytechnic
36 Collegiate Crescent
Sheffield 10 2BP
Tel: 0742-665274

Bell, Gordon H.
Supervisors: Bell, Gordon H.;
Colbeck, Brian (Sunnyside School,
Coulby, Newham)

The Sunnyside Action Inquiry Project.

Background: The project investigated one primary school's policy on the integration of children with special educational needs.
Design: The investigation involved a whole school in researching its own practice over one school year, to produce a systematic and collaborative portrayal of its experience of integrating children with special educational needs into the mainstream curriculum.
Size: The case studied was a 540-place, five- to eleven-year old primary school with a 40-place nursery class within the building. Included in this provision were places for 30 educationally sub-normal children (ESN(M)), 20 partially hearing children and 10 visually handicapped pupils, plus 10 children attending an adjustment class.
Methods: Action research and case study on a whole-school basis.

Results: The methods adopted were successfuly implemented and led to the development of a series of reports of the work of practitioner research groups within the school. This material provided the focus for policy study with a view to school improvement. Efforts are now being directed to the transfer of this knowledge and experience to other practitioners.

Date of Research: July 1982–January 1985.

Published Material: BELL, G.H. and COLBECK, B. (1984). 'Whole School Practitioner Research: The Sunnyside Action Inquiry Project', *Educational Research*, **26,** 2 June 1984, pp. 88–94.

KEYWORDS: integration; whole school; teacher-based research; ESN(M); partial hearing; visual impairment; primary

1/151   Department of Education
Sheffield City Polytechnic
36 Collegiate Crescent
Sheffield 10 2BP
Tel: 0742-665274

Shoesmith, Sharon, Mrs
Supervisors: Cashdan, A. (Dept. of
Communication Studies); Preston,
M. J., Mrs (Dept, of Education)

Meeting special educational needs in the first school.

Background: Children who fail in the first school do so not through a deficit model but rather as a consequence of self concept and attributional problems. Aim to investigate this hypothesis.
Design: Failing and succeeding pupils identified for three experimental groups, four classes in first schools. Treatment is counselling to influence child's attribution of success and failure.
Size: Small sample taken from four schools – mainly in disadvantaged areas in a northern city.
Methods: Standardized testing; investigations of attribution; observational techniques; counselling.

Date of Research: January 1984–1987.

KEYWORDS: self-concept; counselling; failing pupils; primary.

Sheffield Education Department

1/152   Sheffield Education Department   Garforth, Joan, Miss; Robbins,
              PO Box 67   Stan; Lindsay, Geoff, Dr; Pegge,
              Leopold Street   Brenda, Mrs
              Sheffield S1 1RJ   *Supervisor:* Wilcox, B.
              Tel: 0742-26341

Register of research in Sheffield – special educational needs.

Background: To keep an up-to-date data bank of special needs research being sponsored/supported by the LEA.
Design: A Special Educational Needs Research Monitoring Group has been established.

Date of Research: 1984 (and retrospective collection of data) – Ongoing.

Published Material: SHEFFIELD EDUCATION DEPARTMENT. (1983). *Computers in Special Education.*
ALLASON, C.H., (1984). *School to working life – pupils with special needs.* York: University of York. Centre for Study of Comprehensive Schools, March.

KEYWORDS: register; teacher-based research

Sheffield University

1/153   Department of Linguistics   Treharne, Dilys A., Miss
              University of Sheffield
              Sheffield S10 2TN
              Tel: 0742-78555 ext. 4871

Language assessment of visually handicapped children.

Background: Very few assessments are available for visually handicapped children. Those that are do not provide an adequate evaluation of the child's language. The present research is aimed at providing both a screening test and an in-depth assessment on which to base language therapy. It is hoped to follow this up with a programme of language teaching.

Date of Research: 1981–1986.

KEYWORDS: visual impairment, assessment; language

1/154   Department of Linguistics   Treharne, Dilys A., Miss
              University of Sheffield
              Sheffield S10 2TN
              Tel: 0742-78555 ext. 4871

Language screening test for health visitors and nursery staff.

Background: Health visitors and nursery staff are uncertain when they should refer a child for speech therapy. This test is designed to be used by professionals not specifically trained in speech and language to enable them to find children who need fuller investigation of their language skills.

Design: Test deals with:
Comprehension of Spoken Language
Expression of Spoken Language
Speech Sounds
from 18 months to 4 years.

Size: Relatively small, probably no more than 20 children in each 6-month age band. Total 120.

Methods: Children are assessed on both the screening test and a standardized fuller language test.

Results: So far the correlation between the screen and the standardized test is very high.

Date of Research: April 1984–October 1984.

KEYWORDS: language screening; health visitors; speech therapy; assessment; pre-school

1/155   Division and Institute of Education   Topping, Keith J.
University of Sheffield
Sheffield S10 2TN
Tel: 0742-78555

Paired reading: parameters of effectiveness.

Background: Paired reading is a simple technique for parents and children to use at home to accelerate reading progress. It produces striking effects in motivation, confidence and comprehension, with high cost-effectiveness. Kirklees has established a five-year project to disseminate the technique across the LEA. This presents an unrivalled opportunity for research into the parameters of effectiveness, in the short and long term.

Design: Of the scores of schools involved, some will be selected for more intensive research. These will be large schools running schemes involving large numbers of pupils. In addition, data from many small schools will be aggregated to elicit general trends.

Methods: Individual and group norm-referenced tests, criterion-referenced and curriculum-based assessments, behavioural checklists completed by relevant participants, interviews and questionnaires, etc.

Results: Ongoing. Method so far demonstrated effective with age range 6–14 years, ESN(M) pupils to 'dyslexic' pupils, all ethnic minority groups, all levels of socio-economic status.

Date of Research: December 1983–December 1987.

Published Material: TOPPING, K.J. (1984a). 'Paired Reading: a way to help parents promote children's reading development', *Child Education*, December 1984.
TOPPING, K.J. (1984b). 'Paired Reading: setting up a school-based project', *Child Education*, January 1984.
TOPPING, K.J. (1984c). 'Paired Reading: a parent-powered technique for special needs children', *Special Education: Forward Trends*, **11**, 3.
TOPPING, K.J. (1984d). Paired Reading Training Pack. Huddersfield: Kirklees Psychological Service.

TOPPING, K.J., and WOLFENDALE, S.W. (1985). *Parental Involvement in Children's Reading*. Beckenham: Croom Helm. (In preparation, to press December 1984.)

KEYWORDS: parent teaching; reading; paired reading; programme evaluation; ESN(M); dyslexia

Sir Wilfred Sheldon Children's Centre

1/156   Sir Wilfrid Sheldon Children's Centre   Pollak, M., Dr; Tuchler, Hans
Belgrave Children's Hospital
London SW9
Tel: 01-735-2520

Use of a sequencing and memory apparatus for the diagnosis of learning problems – the Pollak Tapper.

Background: A simple, quick, useful, reliable and pleasant method of testing visual and auditory memory and sequencing skills in children with learning problems.
Design: Already standardized on over 500 children in South London and Central Nottinghamshire, and follow-up on the majority.
Methods: One-to-one testing.

Results: 1) Pollak Tapper was reliable.
2) It showed whether the problem was in visual or auditory perception.
3) It had a predictive value.
4) It also showed children with emotional problems.

Date of Research: January 1982–Ongoing.

Published Material: POLLAK, M. and TUCHLER, H. (1982). 'The Pollak Tapper', *Head Teachers Review*, Summer, pp. 19–20.

KEYWORDS: mental handicap; resources; special school survey; parental attitudes; severe learning difficulties; teacher/pupil ratio

Polytechnic of the South Bank

1/157   Faculty of Education, Human and   Mongon, Denis
Social Studies   *Supervisor:* Frampton, D.
Polytechnic of the South Bank
Borough Road
London SE1 0AA
Tel: 01-928-8989

An analysis of the process through which pupils become classified as 'maladjusted' in the education system and consideration of the implications thereof.

Background: This study concerns the processes by which pupils were 'ascertained as maladjusted' before the implementation of the 1981 Education Act. Despite changes in the law and practice, the strength of professional interests and the relative powerlessness of pupils and parents mean that the referral of such pupils under some description to some form of special provision is likely to persist.

Design: An historical review defines the subject and two main themes: the continual dominance of a medical model; and the fluctuating pre-eminence of different professional groups. The study is then linked to the sociology of education. Weber's typology of 'class, status and power' is selected to 'catalogue' groups and introduce other sociological perspectives.

Methods: (1) Examining the referral papers of 163 ascertained pupils,
(2) Interviewing a senior staff member at a sample of 15 schools identified in (1)
(3) Using relevant literature to support the analysis of (1) and (2).
Personal data, referral rationales from the documents, interview responses to questions about the data and answers concerning institutional reactions are all reported in detail. These are then analysed with associated material under four headings: professional values; the ecology of maladjustment; social class; gender and ethnicity.

Date of Research: September 1978–April 1984.

Published Material: FORD, J., MONGON, D. and WHELAN, M. (1982). *Special Education and Social Control.* London: Routledge and Kegan Paul.

KEYWORDS: hearing impairment; social skills; training; interaction; adolescence

Spastics Society

1/158   Department of Educational and   Jernquist, Lillemor; Stukat, Karl-
        Social Studies   Gustaf, Prof.
        The Spastics Society
        16 Fitzroy Square
        London W1
        Tel: 01-387-9571 ext. 237

Speech regulation of motor acts: experimental studies of a key feature of conductive education.

Background: Conductive education is used in the UK in some 25 schools and is increasingly popular. 'Rhythmical intention' – the method of linking speech and movement – has two aspects: 1) the instruction given; 2) the child's co-ordination of speech and movement. These two aspects are in focus.

Design: Manipulation of the two aspects of rhythmical intention: (a) three modes of instruction (gestural, gestural and verbal, verbal), two degrees of task difficulty tried on children in four different stages of speech regulation; (b) co-ordination of speech-movement-motor and semantic. Aspects of speech are manipulated.

Size: 48 cerebral palsied children; C.A. 2–8 years; M.A. 1–8 years.

Methods: Observation and experimental tasks.

Results: Under preparation.

Date of Research: 1982–1984

KEYWORDS: cerebral palsy; speech regulation; motor skills; conductive education

Strathclyde University

1/159   Department of Psychology   Swanson, W.I.
University of Strathclyde
155 George Street
Glasgow
Tel: 041-552-4400

The social and educational adjustment of physically handicapped pupils in primary schools.

Background: Aim was to provide information on the way in which physically handicapped pupils cope in normal primary school environments.
Design: A variety of data was gathered: IQ and educational achievement of sample; information from teachers *re* social integration; structured interview data from parents; pupil responses *re* personality and adjustment.
Size: Small group
Methods: Interview, standardized tests.

Results: A number of issues were illuminated as a result of the investigation, i.e. the role of the 'caring' agencies, the expectations of the handicapped and their families, the influence of teachers' views.

Date of Research: November 1982–April 1983.

Published Material: SWANSON, I.W. and O'HAGAN, F.J. (1983). 'Teachers' views regarding the role of the educational psychologist in schools', *Res. Educ.*, 29, May 1983, pp. 29–40.

KEYWORDS: physical handicap; primary; integration; social adjustment

London Borough of Sutton

1/160   Education Department   Turner, G.C. (Sutton Headteacher
London Borough of Sutton   – Camden Junior School);
The Grove   Wincott, G. (Norfolk Headteacher
Cashalton   – Wells-by-Sea, C.P. School)
Surrey SM5
Tel: 01-661-5000

Teachers' expecations of in-service training provision (particular reference to special education).

Background: With the implementation of the 1981 Education Act there will be a need to develop a greater awareness and understanding of children with special educational needs amongst all teachers in ordinary schools. A simple survey devised to discover some of the attitudes and expectations of teachers towards in-service training, especially in the area of special education.
Design: Simple questionnaire – nine questions.
Size: 200 questionnaires circulated through seven mainly 'East Anglian' Authorities (L.B. of Sutton the exception). 116 replies.
Methods: Distribution and collection of questionnaire arranged through the co-operation of fellow members of the Cambridge Institute Course.

Results: Various conclusions, including (a) Teachers' general satisfaction with much INSET; (b) Importance placed on early identification of special needs.

Date of Research: February 1984–March 1984.

KEYWORDS: in-service education

Thomas Coram Research Unit

See under London University.

Trent Polytechnic

1/161   Department of Physical Science   Jones, Alan V.
           Trent Polytechnic
           Clifton
           Nottingham NG11 8NS
           Tel: 0602-418248

Teaching science to handicapped pupils.

Background: 1) To produce relevant and tested practical science and technological activities for handicapped pupils. 2) To encourage teachers to do science activities with handicapped pupils.

Design: Advice was given to the project leaders by practising teachers and educators.

Results: This is an ongoing project but some of the findings can be found in the publications listed below. Further work involves producing a book for teacher trainers.

Date of Research: 1979–Ongoing.

Published Material: JONES, A.V. (1983a). 'Integration of Handicapped Pupils into Normal School and Particularly into Science Lessons', *Education in Science*, 105, Nov. 1983, pp. 31–2.
JONES, A.V. (1983b). *Science for Handicapped Children.* London: Souvenir Press.
DEWSBURY, M. and JONES, A.V. (1984). 'Science Teaching at the Bedside', *Special Educ: Forward Trends*, **11**, 1, pp. 35–7.
JONES, A.V. *et al.* (1984). 'Science with Handicapped Pupils', *Physics Education*, **19**, pp. 6–10.
JONES, A.V. (1984). 'Teaching Handicapped Pupils', *Education in Chemistry*, **21**, 2, March, p. 40.

KEYWORDS: science teaching; teacher training

University of Ulster

1/162   University of Ulster   Beech, John R., Dr; Harding,
           Coleraine BT52 1SA   Leonora M., Dr
           Northern Ireland
           Tel: 0265-4141

Phonemic processing and the backward reader from a developmental lag viewpoint.

Background: The experiment investigated whether there was a developmental lag in skills associated with phonemic processing in backward readers of normal non-verbal intelligence. Also the relationship between phonemic processing and reading style was investigated.
Design: Essentially, backward readers reading age controls and chronological age controls were compared in tests of phonemic processing.
Size: Fifty-seven backward readers, 44 younger readers of the same reading level and 35 normal readers of the same age as the backward readers were given tests involving phonemic processing and memory. The subjects were drawn from four schools in the Coleraine area.
Methods: The tests that were given included: Wepman auditory discrimination; speech; rhyme recognition; odd word out task; digit span; word memory; reading style test.

Results: In virtually all these tests involving phonemic processing including phonemic discrimination and speech tests, the backward readers were significantly worse than the chronological age controls, but there was no difference between the backward readers and the reading age controls.
   There was little evidence for a relationship between phonemic processing and reading style and there were no differences in reading style between the three groups.

Date of Research: March 1982–September 1982.

Published Material: BEECH, J.R. and HARDING, L.M. (1984). 'Phonemic processing and the backward reader from a developmental lag viewpoint', *Reading Research Quarterly* (in press).

KEYWORDS: phonemic processing; developmental lag; speech; memory; backward reader; reading style

1/163   The Education Centre   Harding, Leonora M., Dr
               University of Ulster   *Supervisor:* Nesbitt, J. Prof.
               Coleraine BT52 1SA
               Northern reland
               Tel: 0265-4141

The relationship between reading ability and development levels in primary school children.

Background: This study aimed to examine developmental lag and other factors within specific reading disability in $7\frac{1}{2}$- to $8\frac{1}{2}$-year-old children.
Design: A $2 \times 2 \times 2$ factorial design was employed, dividing children by reading ability (average readers, mean R.A. 9–0 years, versus reading disabled, mean R.A. 6–3 years), sex (boys versus girls) and class (middle class versus working class). The children were of average intelligence (mean WISC 103.4).
Size: Twenty-four reading disabled children and 24 average readers of between $7\frac{1}{2}$ and $8\frac{1}{2}$ years of age were taken from a random sample of 13 schools out of a possible 61 in an area of Northern Ireland.
Methods: Forth-three measures relating to development as well as 18 measures of reading and spelling skills were taken for each child. An 18-item questionnaire relating to home background was given to the parents. Analysis was by analysis of variance and chi-square.

Results: In most measures reading disabled children were significantly poorer than normals. This result gives qualified support for the developmental lag hypothesis.

There were few main sex or class differences but reading disabled boys would seem to constitute a more severely backward subgroup.

The environment may be an exacerbating factor for such children, who also adopt a reading-for-meaning style.

Date of Research: 1977–March 1983.

Published Material: LEMON, L.M. (1981). Specific reading disability. The difference between the sexes. Proceedings of the 5th Annual Conference of the Reading Association of Ireland, Dublin.
LEMON, L.M. (1982). 'Language development and reading errors in children with specific reading disability', *British Psychological Society Bulletin*, **35,** 117.
HARDING, L.M. (1984). 'Reading errors and reading style in children with a specific reading disability', *Journal of Research in Reading* (in press).

KEYWORDS: Reading disability; dyslexia; developmental lag; miscue; home background; sex differences; primary

Ulster University

1/164   University of Ulster at Jordanstown   Dwyer, Eamonn, Dr; Hargie,
              Shore Road   Owen, Dr
              Newtonabbey
              Co Antrim BT37 0QB
              Tel: 0231-65131

Micro-teaching in the training of instructors of mentally handicapped adults.

Background: A very large number of instructors of mentally handicapped adults in Northern Ireland have no qualifications or formal training in mental handicap. The aim of the research was to evaluate the effectiveness of a programme of microteaching carried out with groups of instructors.
Design: A specially designed 'package' of microteaching skills was developed and taught over a period of six weeks (half day per week).

Skills chosen were: stimulus variation; reinforcement; question; explanation/demonstration.
Size: 35 + instructors of mentally handicapped adults in Northern Ireland.
Methods: The instructors, who had no formal qualifications in working with mentally handicapped adults, undertook a six session (24 hours in total) course in microteaching. Six months approximately after completing the course the participants' views on the value and effectiveness of the course.

Results: The responses collected to date indicate a positive attitude towards microteaching as a training period.

Date of Research: January 1982–January 1985.

Published Material: DWYER, E. and HARGIE, O. (1984). 'The Role of Microteaching in the Training of Instructors of Mental Handicapped Adults: initial report', *International Journal of Rehabilitation Research*, **7,** 1.

KEYWORDS: microteaching; instructors; social skills training; programme evaluation; in-service education; mental handicap; adult

1/165   Faculty of Education   Dwyer, Eamonn, Dr; Swann, Will
           University of Ulster at Jordanstown   (Faculty of Educational Studies,
           Shore Road   Open University)
           Newtownabbey
           Co Antrim BT37 0QB
           Tel: 0231-65131

An investigation of the educational resources available to mentally handicapped children in Northern Ireland, and of the parents' perceptions of the effectiveness of these resources.

Background: Mentally handicapped children in Northern Ireland are excluded from schools within the responsibility of the Department of Education and they attend schools run by Health and Social Service Boards. The survey was designed to investigate the effectiveness of the schools and to seek parents' views on this issue.

Design: This is the most comprehensive investigation of special education ever undertaken in Northern Ireland. (The Warnock Report did not include schools in Northern Ireland.).

Size: (i) 21 schools for mentally handicapped children in Northern Ireland (out of a total of 22) and one Social Education Centre which caters for a very small number of children.

(ii) 17 ESN schools in Northern Ireland (out of a total of 19) and two schools for physically handicapped children (out of two).

(iii) A sample of 20 comparable schools in England.

(iv) 30 + parents of mentally handicapped children in Northern Ireland.

Methods: Survey: (i) Comprehensive questionnaire administered to headteachers of all but one of the schools for the mentally handicapped in Northern Ireland; (ii) abridged version of questionnaire administered to other special schools in Northern Ireland and to sample of special schools in England; (iii) sample of parents of mentally handicapped children in Northern Ireland interviewed.

Results: Initial results show that schools for mentally handicapped children in Northern Ireland are significantly less well resourced than similar schools in England, particularly in terms of teacher/pupil ratio and class assistant pupil ratio. The transport system in Northern Ireland for mentally handicapped children presents serious problems, and accommodation in schools may be having a detrimental effect on the curriculum.

Date of Research: April 1982–April 1985.

Published Material: DWYER, E., SWANN, W. and WOODSIDE, S. 'Provision for Mentally Handicapped Children in Northern Ireland'. In: *New Frontiers*. Report of the National Conference of the National Council for Special Education. Stratford-upon-Avon: N.C.S.E.

DWYER, E. and SWANN, W. The Education of Mentally Handicapped Children in Northern Ireland, Preliminary Report parts 1 and 2. Ulster Polytechnic Mimeo (available from E. Dwyer).

KEYWORDS: mental handicap; resources; special school survey; parental attitudes; severe learning difficulties; teacher/pupil ratio

1/166   Department of Psychology   Phoenix, Susan, Mrs
           University of Ulster at Jordanstown   *Supervisor:* Whittington, Dorothy,
           Shore Road   Miss
           Newtownabbey
           Co Antrim BT37 0QB
           Tel: 0231-65131

Short term social skill training with five profoundly deaf adolescents.

Background: The lack of social skills and appropriate communication skills in young deaf people has been neglected in services to the deaf in Northern Ireland. Recent emphasis upon lack of communication at all stages of deaf children's life suggested need to plan social skills training (SST) programme for deaf school children, especially those falling into the ESN category.

Design: A nine-week programme was devised for group work to develop group problem-solving skills. This was hypothesized to increase positive interaction and decrease negative aggressive behaviour.

Size: Five boys (mean age: 14 years). All attending a school for the deaf. Mean level of deafness: 87·25 db.

Methods: Training as above; assessment was by (1) observations of two problem-solving tasks using video pre and post SST (tasks selected for cooperative work); (2) sociometric analysis of peer group likes/dislikes; (3) questionnaire administration to parents, teachers and housemothers to measure interactional behaviour.

Results: Short term SST will improve positive group interaction and decrease negative behaviour. Teaching staff reported increased 'attending' behaviour, communication skills were observed to improve (although not tested for). It is suggested that such programmes be included in curricular strategies for all hearing impaired children to facilitate developing deaf child's deficits in socialisation process.

Date of Research: October 1982–April 1983.

Published Material: PHOENIX, S. (1983). Short term SST with 5 profoundly deaf adolescent boys. Undergraduate thesis, Ulster Polytechnic.

KEYWORDS: *hearing impairment; social skills; training; interaction; adolescence*

1/167   Department of Special Education   O'Hanlon, Christine, Ms
           Faculty of Education   *Supervisors:* McConkey, Roy, Dr;
           University of Ulster at Jordanstown   Dwyer, Eamonn, Dr
           Shore Road
           Newtownabbey
           Co. Antrim BT37 0QB
           Tel: 0231-65131

Parental perception of available services for parents of mentally handicapped children under five years of age in Belfast.

Background: To ascertain and evaluate the degree and extent of educational and care services available to pre-school mentally handicapped children in North and West Belfast with particular reference to parental perceptions of the efficiency and effectiveness of the services, and to set out a framework for the future development of the services within the context of educational provision.

Size: Parents of approximately 50 mentally handicapped pre-school children.

Methods: The main technique will be the use of interviews, particularly interviews with a sample of parents of mentally handicapped children. A review of literature, analysis and evaluation of data, and proposals for the development of services will also form elements in the project.

Date of Research: September 1982–March 1985.

Published Material: O'HANLON, C. (1984). Provision for education of pre-school mentally handicapped children in Northern Ireland. Paper presented at the 1984 Annual Conference of the National Council for Special Education.

KEYWORDS: mental handicap; nursery provision; parental perception; pre-school; educational provision; parents

University of Wales

1/168   School of Education   Lowden, G., Dr
           University College of North Wales
           Lon Pobty
           Bangor
           Gwynedd LL57 1DZ
           Tel: 0248–351151

The integration of educationally subnormal children in primary schools in Wales.

Background: 1) To examine the attitudes of teachers and mainstream children toward slow learners in primary schools. 2) To identify the forms of organization in the schools and to assess the incidence of 'integration'.

Design: 1) Attitudes: (a) Attitudes of teachers toward slow learners; relationships between mainstream and Unit teachers; differences between teachers in Units for slow learners and mainstream teachers. (b) Reported attitudes of mainstream pupils toward slow learners and vice versa; the extent of 'name-calling' and rejection of slow learners; the attitudes to school of slow learners.

2) Organization of integration: Current practices, forms of organization, incidence; the participation of mainstream teachers in Unit activities and vice versa; Unit entry and secondary transfer arrangements; characteristics of Units.

Size: 759 children in units. 31 children in ordinary classes.

Results: Most teachers preferred not to teach slow learners and thought that the children should be the responsibility of the Unit Teacher. Relationships with Unit Teachers were usually reported as being good. There was little interchange of mainstream and Unit staff. Most teachers deemed integration desirable but impracticable, the ease of integration varying inversely with the 'academic' rating of a curriculum area. There was a general consensus of opinion that a slow learner should be integrated as soon as he showed readiness, but there was little evidence of this happening.

Very little mainstream antagonism towards slow learners was reported on the part of children, staff, and parents: a quarter of the schools actually reported that their mainstream children were 'markedly supportive', and although there were significant differences against slow learners in both acceptance and rejection in class, these were not gross and the most rejected children in the sample came from the mainstream. Slow learners were not markedly inferior to mainstream children in school attitudes, apart from the one factor of 'academic self-image'.

Date of Research: September 1976–September 1983.

Published Material: The Integration of educationally subnormal children in primary schools in Wales. Ph.D thesis, University College of North Wales, Bangor (1983). (Available from the National Library of Wales, Aberystwyth, Dyfed.)
'Integrating slow learners in Wales', *Special Education: Forward Trends*, December 1984, **11**, 4.

KEYWORDS: integration; primary; Wales; moderate learning difficulties; teacher attitude

1/169   School of Education   Williams, Phillip, Prof.
      University College of North Wales
      Lon Pobty
      Bangor
      Gwynedd LL57 1DZ
      Tel: 0248–351151

Glossary of special education.

Background: Aims to provide readily accessible definitions and explanations of terms in general use in special education.
Methods: Computer based indexing and filing.

Date of Research: March 1983–March 1985.

KEYWORDS: glossary; dictionary

1/170   Department of Psychology   Miles, T.R., Prof.
      University College of North Wales
      Lon Pobty
      Bangor
      Gwynedd LL57 2DG
      Tel: 0248–351151

Speed of processing of symbolic information in dyslexic children and adults.

Background: The research began with clinical observation, but it is now necessary to compare the performance of dyslexic and non-dyslexic subjects in more rigorously controlled conditions.
Design: A variety of tasks are being given to dyslexic and non-dyslexic subjects in which they are required to process symbolic and non-symbolic material as rapidly as possible.
Methods: Times and error rates are recorded.

Results: Older dyslexic persons can largely avoid errors if they take sufficient time. Even at student level, however, they continue to be slow at processing symbolic information.

Date of Research: Ongoing.

Published Material: MILES, T.R. (1983). 'On the persistence of dyslexic difficulties into adulthood'. In: Chinn, S.J., Bath, J. & Knox, D. (eds) *Dyslexia Research and Its Applications to the Adolescent*. Bath: Better Books.

KEYWORDS: dyslexia; information processing

1/171   Department of Education   Palmer, J.W., Mrs
      University College, Cardiff   *Supervisor:* Upton, Graham, Dr
      Cathay Park
      PO Box 78
      Cardiff CF1 1XL
      Tel: 0222-44211

A comparative study of the teaching of social academic skills in social education centres.

Background: In the rapidly developing field of mental handicap the role of staff in ATC is becoming even more difficult to define. The increase in the number of 'relevant' courses for MH people in FE colleges is adding to the confusion. This piece of work sets out to examine this scene.

Design: An examination of the allocation of responsibility for teaching social academic skills in ATC/SEC in Wales and the S. West to determine to what extent such teaching is seen as an integral part of the programme of overall development of MH people.

Size: Approximately 30 ATC/SEC. Age-range of population to be included – 16–25 years.

Methods: *Stage 1* Questionnaire to identify the pattern (or lack of pattern) in the allocation of responsibility for teaching social academic skills and the philosophy on which the practice is based.

Stage 2 Questionnaire followed by visits, if necessary, to a representative sample of SEC/ATC to explore the relevance of the programme to meeting the overall aims of the SEC/ATC.

Date of Research: October 1982–June 1987.

KEYWORDS: mental handicap; continuing education; severe learning difficulties; adult training centre; social education centre

1/172	Department of Education Annex	Harris, John, Dr
	University College, Cardiff	
	66, Park Place	
	Cardiff CF1 1XL	

A survey of language teaching in special schools (ESNS) in Wales.

Background: Since very little material has been published concerned with how teachers of mentally handicapped children approach the problem of language teaching, this study is designed to provide information regarding the organization of teaching groups, language assessment and language teaching.

Design: Survey of teachers and headteachers in special schools (ESNS) in Wales.

Size: Schools – 34
Headteachers – 34
Class teachers – 102

Methods: Questionnaire.

Date of Research: January 1983–Autumn 1984 (provisional).

KEYWORDS: special school survey; language teaching; ESN(S); language assessment.

1/173	Sociological Research Unit	Rees, Teresa L., Ms; Atkinson,
	University College, Cardiff	Paul, Dr
	Cathay Park	
	PO Box 78	
	Cardiff CF1 1XL	
	Tel: 0222–44211 ext. 255	

Evaluation of industrial training units for slow learners.

Background: A S. Wales LEA set up six Industrial Training Units to prepare slow learners for working life. They became an associated project in the EEC's Action Programme on the Transition from School to Working Life and were evaluated by the Sociological Research Unit.

Design: The evaluation focused on the *processes* of learning and interaction within the units, and *products*, that is to what extent the students did achieve open employment. In addition, a series of studies served to *locate* the Units in the structures of policy and provision for the handicapped locally and nationally and the context of the deteriorating local labour market and increase in state intervention in the general area of transition from school to work.

Size: The entire cohort of students in two Units were observed and others studied through analysis of careers records.

Methods: The nature of the client group precluded the possibility of the usual interview or questionnaire techniques. The methodology of the evaluation therefore combined a range of techniques. Most of it comprised observation and reconstruction of everyday life in two Units. In addition an analysis of student records charted their transition from school, through the units and into the labour market. Finally, in depth interviews were conducted with a wide range of 'actors' in the transition from head teachers of special schools, staff of the units, careers officers, local employers and so on.

Results: The results of the evaluation demonstrated the difficulties of such a programme being effective in achieving its aims in a context of declining job opportunities. Structural changes in the economy have reduced the number of kinds of jobs to which slow learners may realistically aspire. At the same time the rise in youth unemployment has led to an increase in the number of special programmes for all school leavers: thus diminishing whatever gain in competitive edge the Units may have given the slow learners. The worsening context in which the Units operate has to a certain extent clouded the pedagogic issues that they raise.

Date of Research: October 1979 – February 1983.

Published Material: The evaluation has been written up in great detail in a series of 16 reports, 3 published monographs and 4 chapters in books: a complete list is available from the author.

a) Monographs:

DOOGAN, K.A. (1982). *Follow-up of Disadvantaged Job Seekers: the Careers of the Trainees of the Bridgend and Merthyr Tydfil Industrial Training Units.* Cologne: IFAPLAN.

ELLIS, R. (1982). *Industrial Units for Slow Learners in Mid Glamorgan.* Cologne: IFAPLAN.

SHONE, D. and ATKINSON, P. (1982). *Everyday Life in Two Industrial Training Units.* Cologne: IFAPLAN.

b) Contributions in books and journals:

SHONE, D. & ATKINSON, P. (1981). 'Industrial Training for Slow Learners: an ethnographic study', *Education for Development*, **6**, 3, April, pp. 25 – 30.

ATKINSON, P., REES, T.L. & SHONE, D. (1982). 'Labouring to Learn? Industrial Training for Slow Learners'. In: Barton, L. & Tomlinson, S. (eds) *Special Education: Policy, Practices and Social Issues.* London: Harper & Row.

ATKINSON, P., REES, T.L. & SHONE, D. (1983). 'Industrial Training for the Disadvantaged'. In: Gleeson, D. (ed) *Youth Training and the Search for Work: A Study of Young People in Crisis.* London: Routledge and Kegan Paul.

REES, T.L. (1984). 'Slow Learners: From Special Education to Special Programmes'. In: Varlaam, C. (ed) *Rethinking Transition: Educational Innovation and the Transition to Adult Life.* Sussex: Falmer Press.

DOOGAN, K. (1984). 'Disadvantaged Youth in the Pursuit of Work'. In: Varlaam, C. (ed) *Rethinking Transition: Educational Innovation and the Transition to Adult Life.* Sussex: Falmer Press.

KEYWORDS: industrial training unit; slow learner; EEC action programme; open employment; labour market; transition to adult life

1/174   Department of Education   Carroll, H.C.M.
University College of Swansea   *Supervisor:* Chazan, M., Prof.
Hendrefoilan
Swansea SA2 7NB
Tel: 0792-201231

Primary school pupils with poor attendance records: a study of seven- and eleven-year-old children and their home and school environments.

Background: Pupil absenteeism in the primary school has received little attention from researchers – hence the study. It aims to examine the medical, social and educational causes of such absenteeism and to determine its possible effects.
Design: The investigation is based on data from two surveys:
(a) The National Child Development Study – data gathered at birth, 7 years and 11 years;
(b) A cross-sectional study of 10/11-year-olds in a single local authority.
Size: Survey (a) 7513 children born in March 1958 in England, Wales and Scotland, being a representative sample of the NCDS 1958 cohort. (b) 273 10/11 years from one LEA in South Wales.
Methods: Children with poor attendance (% attendance less than 81) in *both* top infants (aged 6/7 years) and top juniors (aged 10/11 years) compared with children with better attendance records. Data analysed using univariate and multivariate nonparametric and parametric techniques.

Results: Available in 1985.

Date of Research: October 1976–October 1984.

KEYWORDS: pupil absenteeism; National Child Development Study; longitudinal; primary

1/175   Institute of Health Care Studies   Shepperdson, Billie, Mrs
University College of Swansea
Singleton Park
Swansea SA2 8PP
Tel: 0792-205678 ext. 5313

A follow up and comparative study of Down's syndrome children and their families in South Wales.

Background: In 1972 a study was made of Down's syndrome children in South Wales living at home who were born in 1964, 1965 and 1966. Two studies based on this earlier research are being carried out. The focus in the research is on identifying differences within the population of Down's syndrome children and their families and not on comparisons with the normal population.
Design: In the 1970s there has been a marked improvement in services to the handicapped. This study sets out to see if these services have actually worked and have resulted in improvements in the adjustment and satisfaction levels of mothers and in the achievements of the children.
Size: A new sample of all Down's syndrome children living at home in South Wales and born in the years 1973, 1974 and 1975 has been identified.
Methods: Psychometric assessment of children. Parent interviews.

Date of Research: April 1981–September 1984.

Published Material: 'Abortion and euthanasia of Down's Syndrome children – the parents' view', *J. Med. Ethics*, 1983, 9, 152–7.

'Waren Sie für Euthanasie', *Medical Tribune*, November 1983. *Families with Down's Syndrome children: a summary of the main findings.* School of Social Studies, University College of Swansea (forthcoming).
'Care of Downs Syndrome teenagers', *Update*, February 1984, 370.

KEYWORDS: Down's syndrome; services; parents

West Glamorgan Education Department

1/176   West Glamorgan Education   Branston, Peter
               Department
               County Hall
               Swansea SA1 3SN
               Tel: 0792-471111

Parental involvement in early reading.

Background: There is strong evidence of the effect on children's development of the quality of parental/child interaction (Wells, Hewison, Tizard, Wade). This project will study the effect over time of structured parental involvement. The project will be supported by workshops, parent 'clinics', language resource materials and a generous supply of children's books.
Design: A subjective assessment of the gains made by children in the project will be supplemented by criterion referenced assessment and comparison with a matched control group.
Size: Twenty experimental; twenty controls.
Methods: Longitudinal and cross sectional comparisons. The study will continue as pupils go through school.

Results: The hypotheses are that the performance in language and reading studies of the experimental group will be superior to that of the controls, that parental attitudes to and involvement in schools will alter and that early interventions of this kind will substantially reduce the number of pupils with moderate learning difficulties.

Date of Research: September 1984–July 1985.

Published Material: WELLS, C.G. (1982). 'Language Learning and Education'. University of Bristol.
HEWISON, J. (1979). Home Environment and Reading Attainment. Unpublished Ph.D, University of London.

KEYWORDS: parental involvement; reading; moderate learning difficulties

West London Institute of Higher Education

1/177   Department of Education   Sandow, Sarah A., Dr
               West London Institute of Higher
               Education
               300, St. Margarets Road
               Twickenham
               Middlesex TW1 1PT

Parent/professional interaction and the preparation of statements according to the provisions of the 1981 Education Act.

Background: The 1981 Act provides for the interprofessional assessment of children with special needs, with emphasis on parental participation. The process depends on accurate and coinciding perceptions of the process of assessment and its meaning. The programme is designed to investigate parental perceptions of the professionals and the assessment and that of the professionals themselves.

Design: Stage 1: Interviews in outer London of parents of children being assessed.
Stage 2: Use of repertory grid to interview parents + professionals in one borough.
Size: Stage 1: N = 40
Stage 2: N = 10 (pilot) + cohort of 1 year.
Methods: Stage 1: Likert scaled interview[1]
Stage 2: Repertory Grid[2] (pilot) followed by 1 or 2 above as most appropriate.

Date of Research: September 1983–September 1986.

KEYWORDS: parents; professionals; Education Act 1981; assessment; statement; repertory grid

Wiltshire Educational Psychology Service

1/178   Educational Psychology Service   Cowell, David E.
Akers Way
Moredon
Swindon
Wiltshire
Tel: 0793-28852/21284

Screening for counselling and guidance.

Background: A number of counselling approaches in the secondary school have taken a Rogerian view, although a wide variety of types of guidance in comprehensive schools can be noted. It is suggested that there is a need for a screening procedure for counselling and guidance, which would incorporate a range of follow-up options.
Design: A 'problem check-list' has been administered to all new students at a sixth form college, and on two occasions to all new admissions to a secondary school at the 14 + stage.
Size: Several hundred pupils mainly in the Swindon area.
Methods: A problem check-list, followed by a range of options: individual interviews; referral to outside agencies such as educational psychologist, and the involvement of voluntary counsellors either within or outside school.

Results: It seems possible to help many pupils before they present as problems. Furthermore, many with learning, personal, and family problems who would not self-refer can be helped by this procedure. The school is also appropriately seen as a suitable base for the provision of help from a number of professional groups.

Date of Research: 1975–There have been several interim reports; the work is ongoing.

Published Material: COWELL, D.E. (1981). Screening for counselling. Paper read at the Annual Conference of the Association of Educational Psychologists, University of Birmingham, 1981.
COWELL, D. and FRANKLIN, J. (1984). 'Screening for counselling and guidance in the secondary school using a team approach', *AEP Journal*, **6**, 3, Spring, 27–32.

KEYWORDS: screening; counselling; guidance; behaviour problem; secondary

Name Index

Adams, M. 1/049
Agnew, N. Ms 1/035
Akhurst, C.R. 1/105
Allen, J. Dr 1/020
Allinson, O. 1/077
Alston, J. 1/038
Aspin, D. Prof. 1/075
Atkinson, P. Dr 1/173
Badger, B. 1/061
Bailey, I. Mrs 1/056
Barnard, A. Mrs 1/002
Barnes, D. 1/066
Baron-Cohen, S. 1/102
Barry, S. Dr 1/028
Beavers, H. Ms 1/120
Beech, J. Dr 1/162
Bell, G.H. 1/150
Bennett, N. Prof. 1/061 1/062 1/063
Best, R. 1/033
Blythman, M. 1/149
Bookis, J. Miss 1/143
Booth, T. 1/130
Bowler, D. 1/088 1/089
Bowman, I. Mrs 1/077
Bradley, J. Dr 1/111 1/112
Branston, P. 1/176
Braund, M. 1/125
Brinkworth, R. 1/010
Brother Henry 1/100 1/101
Brown, A. 1/142
Brown, M. Dr 1/074
Brown, R. 1/118 1/119
Browning, M. Mrs 1/055 1/056
Bruce, D. Dr 1/031
Buckland, M. Mrs 1/022
Buckley, S. Mrs 1/136
Budge, A. 1/044
Buist, M. Ms 1/041
Bunt, L. 1/049
Buultjens, M. Mrs 1/044
Carroll, H. 1/174
Casey, W. Dr 1/073
Cashdan, A. 1/151
Cawley, N. 1/029
Chambers, M. 1/001
Chazan, M. Prof. 1/174
Cherrington, D. 1/010
Child, J. 1/030
Chinn, S. Dr 1/045
Clayton, B. 1/029

Colbeck, B. 1/150
Combes, G. Ms 1/057
Constable, H. Dr 1/119
Cooper, D. Ms 1/108
Corbett, J. Ms 1/130
Cordes, W. 1/107
Corrie, M. 1/147 1/148
Cowell, D.E. 1/178
Craft, A. Mrs 1/006
Croll, P. 1/022
Cross, G. Dr 1/021
Crystal, D. Prof. 1/141
Cullen, C. Dr 1/094
Daly, G. 1/034
Dance, A. 1/005
Davidson, R. Mrs 1/023 1/025
Davies, J. Mrs 1/053
Dean, A. 1/113
Dee, L. Ms 1/114
Denvir, B. Mrs 1/074
Devereux, K. Mrs 1/103
Dixon, J.K. 1/146
Dunn, W.R. 1/046
Dwyer, E. Dr 1/164 1/165 1/167
Edmonds, M. Ms 1/095
Elliott, C. Dr 1/098
Entwhistle, N. Prof. 1/037
Eskdale, R. 1/137
Evans, J. Ms 1/085
Evans, P. Dr 1/078 1/079
Farrell, P. 1/095 1/097
Foster, G. 1/030
Frampton, D. 1/157
Francis, H. Prof. 1/080
Francis, J. Mrs 1/121
Freeman, A. 1/065
Frith, U. Dr 1/087 1/092 1/102 1/117
Gammage, P. Prof. 1/007
Garforth, J. Miss 1/152
Gipps, C. Dr 1/086
Goacher, B. 1/085
Goldstein, H. Prof. 1/086
Goulding, S. Mrs 1/039
Green, D. Dr 1/032
Green, L. 1/121
Griffiths, J. 1/084
Gross, H. Ms 1/086
Grubb, J. Dr 1/027
Gulliford, R. Prof. 1/016
Hackney, A. Dr 1/135

Subject Index

professionals, repertory grid, statement

ATTAINMENT
1/013 cognition, longitudinal, visual
impairment
1/121 Stott's guide, learning skills, primary,
screening

ATTENTION DEFICIT
1/091 assessment, conduct disorder,
epidemiology, hyperactivity, screening

AUTISM
1/098 British sign language, mental handicap,
non-verbal communication, signing system

AUTISTIC
1/092 adult, cognitive processing, spatial
location, visuo-spatial skills
1/102 Down's syndrome, social cognition
1/117 dyslexia, ESN(M), reading,
comprehension
1/139 computer assisted learning,
microcomputer, software

BACKWARD READER
1/162 developmental lag, memory, phonemic
processing, reading style, speech

BACKWARD SPELLER
1/122 Stott's guide, diagnostic spelling test,
longitudinal, reading, spelling

BEGINNING READING
1/080 orthography, reading

BEHAVIOUR CHANGE
1/097 behaviour problem, follow-up study,
mental handicap, severe learning difficulties,
skill deficiency

BEHAVIOUR INVENTORY
1/009 checklist, conduct disorder, screening

BEHAVIOUR MODIFICATION
1/095 EDY course, in-service education,
mental handicap, severe learning difficulties,
teacher training

BEHAVIOUR PROBLEM
1/007 anxiety, learning difficulties
1/008 conduct disorder, family, parent training
1/053 programme evaluation, reintegration,
secondary, support centres
1/061 school processes, secondary
1/097 behaviour change, follow-up study,
mental handicap, severe learning difficulties,
skill deficiency
1/135 in-service education, integration, teacher
training
1/178 counselling, guidance, screening,
secondary

BEHAVIOURAL TEACHING APPROACH
1/099 in-service education, school-focussed
training, training pack

BIBLIOGRAPHY
1/014 Down's syndrome

BLISSYMBOLS
1/128 ESN(S), graphic symbol, mental
handicap, pre-school, reading, symbol
accentuation

BRAILLE
1/017 adult, computer assisted learning,
mathematics, microcomputer, software,
visual impairment, visual perception
1/133 microcomputer, software, synthetic
speech, visual impairment

BRITISH SIGN LANGUAGE
1/098 autism, mental handicap, non-verbal
communication, signing system

CAMP SCHOOL
1/138 crafts

CENTRAL NERVOUS SYSTEM
1/001 dyslexia, information processing

CEREBRAL PALSY
1/104 assessment, longitudinal, multiple
handicap
1/142 assessment, communication,
microcomputer, physical handicap
1/158 conductive education, motor skills,
speech regulation

CHECKLIST
1/009 behaviour inventory, conduct disorder,
screening
1/034 longitudinal, screening
1/038 handwriting, legibility, primary screening

CHESS
1/035 physical handicap

CLASSROOM MANAGEMENT
1/079 cognitive development, severe learning
difficulties, special care unit

CLASSROOM ORGANIZATION
1/134 integration, primary, room management

CODING
1/090 cognitive processing, manual sign
language, mental handicap, signing system

COGNITION
1/013 attainment, longitudinal, visual
impairment
1/083 assessment, development scale,
individualized instruction, multiple handicap,
physical handicap

COGNITIVE DEVELOPMENT
1/021 ESN, Piaget, maturation, social maturity
1/079 classroom management, severe learning
difficulties, special care unit

learning difficulties, special school survey, teacher/pupil ratio
1/167 educational provision, nursery provision, parental perception, parents, pre-school
1/171 adult training centre, continuing education, severe learning difficulties, social education centre

MENTAL RETARDATION
1/036 mentally handicapped adults, reading, special education, teaching method

MENTALLY HANDICAPPED ADULTS
1/036 mental retardation, reading, special education, teaching method

MICROCOMPUTER
1/012 computer equipment, software, special school survey
1/017 adult, Braille, computer assisted learning, mathematics, software, visual impairment, visual perception
1/022 logo
1/032 software, physical handicap, ESN, mathematics, Piaget
1/037 communication aid, computer assisted learning
1/100 adult literacy, software
1/101 dyslexia, short-term memory, software, spelling
1/125 further education, moderate learning difficulties, social education, software
1/132 distance education, hearing impairment, information technology, physical handicap, visual impairment
1/133 Braille, software, synthetic speech, visual impairment
1/139 autistic, computer assisted learning, software
1/140 software
1/142 assessment, cerebral palsy, communication, physical handicap
1/144 hearing impairment, speech display, visual feedback
1/146 ESN(M) schools, curriculum, development, resource centre, in-service education, software, whole school
1/149 computer assisted learning, curriculum development, moderate learning difficulties, software

MICROTEACHING
1/164 adult, in-service education, instructors, mental handicap, programme evaluation, social skills training

MIDDLE SCHOOL
1/137 management, programme evaluation, whole school

MISCUE
1/163 developmental lag, dyslexia, home background, primary, reading disability, sex differences

MODERATE LEARNING DIFFICULTIES
1/062 integration, transfer of pupils

1/068 primary, curriculum development, cognitive strategies
1/078 curriculum development
1/081 ESN(M), aims of education, primary curriculum, teacher training
1/084 curriculum development, organization of knowledge, severe learning difficulties, subnormality hospital
1/111 in-service education, dissemination, further education, staff development
1/112 videotape, in-service education, further education, staff development
1/125 further education, microcomputer, social education, software
1/149 computer assisted learning, curriculum development, microcomputer, software
1/168 Wales, integration, primary, teacher attitude
1/176 parental involvement, reading

MOTOR CONTROL
1/020 Down's syndrome, spatial ability, temporal anticipation

MOTOR IMPAIRMENT
1/042 assessment, physical education, remedial provision

MOTOR PROBLEMS
1/069 assessment, learning difficulties

MOTOR SKILLS
1/158 cerebral palsy, conductive education, speech regulation

MOVEMENT EDUCATION
1/024 Sherborne, teacher training

MULTIDISCIPLINARY
1/046 assessment, deaf/blind, hearing impairment, multiple handicap, sensory impairment, survey
1/055 ESN(S), assessment, curriculum development, severe learning difficulties

MULTIPLE HANDICAP
1/043 soft play equipment, physical handicap
1/046 assessment, deaf/blind, hearing impairment, multidisciplinary, sensory impairment, survey
1/056 assessment, curriculum development, profound mental handicap, severe learning difficulties
1/083 assessment, cognition, development scale, individualized instruction, physical handicap
1/094 conductive education, mental handicap, teacher attitude
1/103 computer, computer assisted learning, counting, numeracy, physical handicap
1/104 assessment, cerebral palsy, longitudinal

MUSCULAR DYSTROPHY
1/107 employment, further education, higher education

MUSIC
1/145 curriculum development, in-service

1/162 backward reader, developmental lag, memory, reading style, speech

PHONOLOGY
1/141 language disorder, linguistic profile

PHYSICAL EDUCATION
1/042 assessment, motor impairment, remedial provision

PHYSICAL HANDICAP
1/004 assessment, educational attainment, visual impairment, visual perception
1/005 driving tuition, neurological damage, perceptual-cognitive skill
1/011 ESN(M) schools, responding skills, teaching approach
1/035 chess
1/043 multiple handicap, soft play equipment
1/060 higher education, school leaver
1/082 personality, repertory grid, residential school, secondary, self concept
1/083 assessment, cognition, development scale, individualized instruction, multiple handicap
1/096 adult, hydrocephalus, integration, neurology, spina bifida
1/103 computer, computer assisted learning, counting, multiple handicap, numeracy
1/126 curriculum development, further education, transition to adult life
1/129 Down's syndrome, curriculum development, depth perception, educational provision, further education, integration, severe learning difficulties
1/130 curriculum development, educational provision, integration, further education
1/131 hearing impairment, information technology, visual impairment
1/132 distance education, hearing impairment, information technology, microcomputer, visual impairment
1/142 assessment, cerebral palsy, communication, microcomputer
1/143 school leaver
1/159 integration, primary, social adjustment

PIAGET
1/021 ESN, cognitive development, maturation, social maturity
1/032 microcomputer, software, physical handicap, ESN, mathematics

PICTORIAL SYMBOL
1/025 reading, rebus, severe learning difficulties, teacher attitude

PLAY
1/040 Down's syndrome, communication, language, primary, severe learning difficulties
1/049 adult, mental handicap, music therapy
1/120 Down's syndrome, pre-school, prelinguistic communication, teacher education, videotape
1/124 deaf/blind, adult, recreation

POLICY
1/044 Education Act 1981, integration, visual impairment
1/085 Education Act 1981, assessment, educational provision
1/086 Education Act 1981, assessment, educational provision, remediation, screening

POLLAK TAPPER
1/156 assessment, memory

PORTAGE
1/039 direct instruction, precision teaching, support service
1/136 Down's syndrome, early education, family, home teaching, pre-school

POST-16
1/108 educational provision, adult, further education, training, EEC
1/113 adult education, further education, severe learning difficulties
1/114 curriculum development, curriculum framework, further education, severe learning difficulties
1/147 further education, leavers' programmes, longitudinal, transition to adult life, vocational education
1/148 adult training centre, further education, provision, training

POST-SCHOOL
1/059 adult training centre, crafts, horticulture, mental handicap, rural studies

PRE-SCHOOL
1/002 assessment, reading, screening, spelling, writing
1/010 Down's syndrome, developmental programme, diet
1/120 Down's syndrome, play, prelinguistic communication, teacher education, videotape
1/128 ESN(S), blissymbols, graphic symbol, mental handicap, reading, symbol accentuation
1/136 Down's syndrome, early education, family, home teaching, portage
1/154 assessment, health visitors, language screening, speech therapy
1/167 educational provision, mental handicap, nursery provision, parental perception, parents

PRECISION TEACHING
1/039 direct instruction, portage, support service

PRELINGUISTIC COMMUNICATION
1/120 Down's syndrome, play, pre-school, teacher education, videotape

PRIMARY
1/015 curriculum development, mathematics, visual impairment
1/030 Education Act 1981, curriculum development, in-service education, named teacher, secondary

mathematics, microcomputer, visual
perception
1/044 Education Act 1981, integration, policy
1/076 assessment, development, optical aids
1/131 hearing impairment, information
technology, physical handicap
1/132 distance education, hearing impairment,
information technology, microcomputer,
physical handicap
1/133 Braille, microcomputer, software,
synthetic speech
1/150 integration, whole school, teacher based
research, ESN(M), partial hearing, primary
1/153 assessment, language

VISUAL PERCEPTION
1/004 assessment, educational attainment,
physical handicap, visual impairment
1/017 adult, Braille, computer assisted learning,
mathematics, microcomputer, software,
visual impairment

VISUO-SPATIAL SKILLS
1/092 adult, autistic, cognitive processing,
spatial location

VOCATIONAL EDUCATION
1/147 further education, leavers' programmes,
longitudinal, post-16, transition to adult life

WALES
1/168 integration, moderate learning
difficulties, primary, teacher attitude

WHOLE SCHOOL
1/137 management, middle school, programme
evaluation
1/146 ESN(M), schools, curriculum
development, resource centre, in-service
education, microcomputer, software
1/150 teacher-based research, ESN(M), partial
hearing, primary, visual impairment,
integration

WRITING
1/002 assessment, pre-school, reading,
screening, spelling

YOUTH TRAINING SCHEME
1/110 school leaver, transition to adult life,
employment, ESN(M)